Richard Watson Dixon

Mano

A poetical history of the time of close of the tenth century concerning the adventures of a Norman knight, which fell part in Normandy, part in Italy; in four books

Richard Watson Dixon

Mano

A poetical history of the time of close of the tenth century concerning the adventures of a Norman knight, which fell part in Normandy, part in Italy; in four books

ISBN/EAN: 9783337292119

Printed in Europe, USA, Canada, Australia, Japan

Cover: Foto ©ninafisch / pixelio.de

More available books at **www.hansebooks.com**

MANO

A POETICAL HISTORY: OF THE TIME OF THE CLOSE OF THE TENTH CENTURY: CONCERNING THE ADVENTURES OF A NORMAN KNIGHT: WHICH FELL PART IN NORMANDY PART IN ITALY.

IN FOUR BOOKS.

BY

RICHARD WATSON DIXON,
VICAR OF HAYTON, HON. CANON OF CARLISLE.

LONDON
GEORGE ROUTLEDGE & SONS
BROADWAY, LUDGATE HILL
NEW YORK: 9 LAFAYETTE PLACE
1883

LONDON:
R. CLAY SONS, AND TAYLOR,
BREAD STREET HILL, E.C.

TO

R. S. B.

THIS POEM IS DEDICATED

BY

R. W. D.

TO THE READER.

This Poem, in the Italian's measure made,
Commended be, if it some deal observe
The law which on his verse the master laid,
   From which the most do in our language swerve,
Who have put forth the triple rime to essay,
(Many of greater name than I deserve :)
   That round the stanza still the structure play,
At end arrested somewhat: this his law,
Who gave such wondrous music to his lay.
   And I, O Reader, filled with hope and awe,
To try the stretched metre of such song,
Shall tell in brief the cause that me did draw.
   Upon occasion given, being then young,
It chanced me to read the histories
Which to the thousandth year from Christ belong.

TO THE READER

Chronicles read I, filled with prodigies,

Wars, tumults, earthquake, famine, pestilence,

Which ran round that dread sum of centuries:

 For all looked that the world should cease from thence,

Then dreadful expectation hung in air,

And excitation quickened mortal sense.

 Wherefore, as in the sunset's reddening glare

The shapes of earth stand stronger on the sky,

So saw I life enhanced, as it were,

 And lifted in that light of misery:

And thought to set my thoughts of man's estate

The better in those colours wild and high:

 To track the dark intricate coils of Fate,

The infinite of pain, the brief of joy,

The better round that far and mystic date.

  And if thou marvel, if thou feel annoy,

Marking how garrulous and low the style

Which for such argument I dare employ,

 Bethink thee of those chroniclers erewhile;

How their thin words drop portents, like a vein

Too weak to hold the blood: and thou wilt smile.

TO THE READER.

For one of them, imagined of their train,
Is for the writer of the history shown,
An old monk, filled with memories of pain.

Herein the stories are not all my own:
But what I found I carried without stint
From every place, nor of that age alone,

But whatso served me best: that so by dint
Of many others might one tale be made:
I took of all, and rolled it in my mint:
Of iron old and new I forged this blade.

CONTENTS.

BOOK I.

CANTO		PAGE
I.	WHAT MOVED FERGANT TO WRITE	1
II.	HOW MANO CAME FROM ITALY	4
III.	HOW SIR MANO DELIVERED HIS LETTERS TO THE DUKE	7
IV.	THE LETTERS OF COUNT THUROLDUS: OTHER LETTERS AND MATTERS SHOWING THE STATE OF THE WORLD	8
V.	OF THE GREATNESS OF THE NORMANS	11
VI.	HOW DUKE RICHARD CAME TO FÉCHAMP	15
VII.	HOW MANO CAST HIS LOVE AT BLANCHE, AND HER SISTER HERS AT HIM	17
VIII.	OF THE CROSSES OF LOVE	20
IX.	HOW BY BLANCHE SIR MANO WAS REFUSED AND MADE FOOLISH	24
X.	HOW JOANNA AND MANO WOULD VISIT GERBERT; AND HOW JOANNA ON THE WAY MET AN OLD PEASANT IN THE FOREST COUNTRY, WHO TOLD HER HIS STORY	26
XI.	THE PEASANT CONTINUES HIS STORY	29

BOOK III.

CANTO		PAGE
I.	How Mano went to Rome	115
II.	What happened in Rome: that Mano was in danger of a Fall	118
III.	The Story of Laurentius and his Children	120
IV.	Mano undertakes the Vengeance of Laurentius's Daughter	123
V.	The Adventure pursued	126
VI.	How Mano was banished by Gerbert	128
VII.	What led Gerbert to misjudge Mano	133
VIII.	Mano parts from Thurold, but not from Fergant	136

BOOK IV.

I.	How Mano and Fergant returned to Normandy	141
II.	Of a strange Dream which came to Fergant	143
III.	How Sir Mano saw Blanche the Fair again	145
IV.	Of a Dream which came to Sir Mano	149
V.	Of the same	151
VI.	How Sir Mano parted from Fergant	152
VII.	How Mano found Diantha with the Peasants in the Wood: and himself was taken by the Lords	154
VIII.	How Diantha fared in Captivity: and how Mano	161
IX.	How Joanna fared in the Convent: and how she discovered Mano's Parentage	164

CONTENTS.

CANTO		PAGE
X.	CONCERNING JOANNA IN THE NUNNERY	167
XI.	HOW JOANNA WENT TO ROUEN TO SAVE SIR MANO, AND HOW SHE SPED	171
XII.	HOW JOANNA CAME TO MANO	176
XIII.	CONCERNING DIANTHA, HOW SHE ESCAPED, AND TO WHAT END SHE CAME	180
XIV.	CONCERNING MANO IN PRISON	184
XV.	THE DEATH OF MANO AND JOANNA	187
XVI.	HOW A FALSE TALE OF THEIR DEATH WAS TOLD, AND THEN THE TRUE: AND HOW THEY WERE BURIED	189
XVII.	THE END	191

BOOK I.

MANO

A POETICAL HISTORY.

BOOK I.

I.—WHAT MOVED FERGANT TO WRITE.

I, FERGANT, living now my latest days,
  Gerbert's disciple once, but long a monk
Of Sant Evreult, for that in many ways
  I have beheld God's strokes upon the trunk
Of rotten trees: and seen the cedars tall
Fall on the hills, because the earth has shrunk
  From nourishing, herself washed down by fall
Of pelting rains, and crumbled by the sun,
So that no state may be perpetual:
  And knowing how things dwindle one by one
To him who clings to this world's misery
Some longer while, ere to the grave he run:
  I, looking soon for that; and since that I

Have seen some things that shall not happen twice,
And days return not that be once gone by:
   And for the cause that many calumnies
Concerning my great Master now be spread,
Gerbert the Pope, that doctor high and wise;
   And of the fate which took him from our head,
And of his arts, his magic spells and songs,
Because that many things be lewdly said:
   And likewise of Sir Mano and his wrongs,
(Who was the friend of Gerbert at the first)
Because that many move their evil tongues;
   For this,—well knowing how they long conversed
In love, till anger rose betwixt them twain,
And by what angry cause their love was cursed:
   I, Fergant, now begin this work of pain,
To vindicate their glory from all foes,
And set the truth in order clear and plain.
         Nor less in duteous memory of those
Who loved my famous master or his friend
Tell I that history, which I marked so close.
   All things shall be recounted, if God send
Strength to this heart, and still with life upstay
The haud that writes, until it reach the end.
         And partly I my master's mind obey,
Who charged me still to hold his memory dear:
Which I refuse not, though, the truth to say,
   Some acts in him of doubtful praise appear;
Nor could my dark mind apprehend the fate
Which cast him suddenly from throne to bier.—
         I, then, if God give aid, shall celebrate
The prodigies, the portents, and events
Of fifty years agone, beginning late:

Yea, great are my concernments and intents
Touching that time, when bursting seemed the earth
With dissolution's sighs and throes and rents
　About the millenary of the Lord's birth:
For we believed that at the thousandth year
The thing would cease in blood and pest and dearth:
　And, as the fatal hour prefixed drew near,
We saw creation cracking, and the signs
Of Antichrist multiplied in our fear.
　For from above depended still the lines
Of God, which heavily the nations beat,
And underneath were laid His secret mines.
　But Gerbert, bold when Nature's shaking seat
The pride of man began to check and quell,
On honour's ladder placed his venturous feet.
　He to the topmost round mounted full well,
And with him to have carried did intend
Sir Mano, who clomb high, but deeply fell.
　For Gerbert, though he counted him his friend,
So soon as once he marked in him defect,
Or thought it, of their friendship made an end:
　He was a man who could a man reject,
And oft required beyond what man could owe:
They who climb honour's hill the sky suspect.
　They who suspect the sky, look not below:
And Gerbert, gazing his high purpose, stood,
Nor pity upon failure would bestow:
　While Mano, who had fierceness in his blood,
At the first question drew himself away;
Woe, for the quarrels of the brave and good!
　This was that Mano who was Thurold's stay,
And in the Italian field the man of note,

Where Thurold had the Normans in his sway.
Mightily played he in those realms remote,
And was in all men's sight uplifted high,
Until dark destiny his voyage smote,
And rent his sail sinful calamity.
But I believe, whatever Gerbert did
Concerning him, when they brake amity,
Was done with pain, albeit the pain was hid.

II.—HOW MANO CAME FROM ITALY.

I DO remember, being in Rouen then
With Gerbert, my grave master in those days,
How Mano came from Italy with men
And letters from Count Thurold; so to raise
For the Count's service succours fresh from home,
And render back to him his warlike praise.
The Normans had been wont at large to roam
Boldly in Italy; but now were pent,
Behind Count Thurold's banner, in their nome.
Thurold had struggled vainly, and was spent:
And now came Mano, his most valiant knight,
To Richard, our young duke, with this intent.
Gerbert received Sir Mano with delight,
And question made, to know how all things were,
And would have had him tarry there the night.
But when Sir Mano doth in terms declare
How quick the post that public need requires,
He bids him on his journey forth to fare:
And I was summoned, at his brief desires,
To be his guide for the remainder way.
Therefore we left behind his knights and squires

And took the road, whither Duke Richard lay
In Lion forest, bent on royal sport :
Thus forth we fared, and made no more delay.
 He seemed a strong young man, of gracious port,
But wondrous pale ; not so full fleshed as those
Whom we had left in hasting to the court—
 The twenty southern knights whom Thurold chose,
Now sitting weary in their armour all
In Rouen ; his features hung together close,
 Making a look most grave ; a heavy fall
Of dark uncurling hair flowed either side :
Upon his horse he sat erect and tall,
 And onward held throughout the toilsome ride
With little speech, though in the thick-set wood
His weary horse oft stumbled in his stride.
 Yet noted I, observing what I could,
Sometimes a fierceness mounted in his eyes,
Or sullen glaze, like to that blinking hood
 Which in the perched owl's orbs by daylight lies :
And oftentimes he sang some little song
Which at the moment in his heart might rise :
 And strangely sent it he the road along,
Though seeming only muttered in his beard :
These things I noted in that warrior strong.
 Moreover, when the way with words we cheered,
Which was not oft, conversing socially,
His laughter like a hurricane I heard.
 Kindly upon me sometimes looked his eye,
But silently amid the solitude
For the more part journeyed the knight and I.
 Alert was he to help me in the wood,
And comfort felt I in his mightiness,

And well I deemed of him, as wise and good.
And when his curving thigh the sell did press,
And his high breast answered his shoulders flat,
Ah, then my lowliness did I confess!
    For doubt rose in me, were I like to that,
So mighty and so swift, so sinewy made,
Whether I should to Christ be dedicate.
    And other thoughts did my sad heart invade,
Of which I make not speech.—Such was this knight,
Who sought from Italy the Norman aid.
    Upon a filly rode a damsel light
Not from his rein a rood, whom he had brought
From Italy: Diantha was she hight;
    Sweet to behold, but yet a thing of naught,
As from this history shall be allowed,
Tyrannous, false, and full of evil thought.
    Thurold's young daughter she, who little showed
Of maidenness, though but of years fifteen,
But with her wildness vexed us on the road.
    For I remember, in the clearings green
Of the thick forest, when we chanced to pass,
If peasant youths standing to gaze were seen,
    Or exercising games upon the grass,
Ready was she to talk with them and jest,
Or drove amidst, as if by chance it was,
    To mock them flying, while the wind abreast
Ruffled her gown, and showed her little shoe.
Often she turned on me, and me distressed,
    So cold her look, her eyes so hard and blue,
Her voice so bitter, and her face so clear.
At times from Mano some rebuke she drew
Which in a scornful silence she would hear.

III.—HOW SIR MANO DELIVERED HIS LETTERS TO THE DUKE.

RIDING we saw about the Lion Wood
  Many pavilions of the following:
And some we passed: then right before us stood
  Another of white silk wide fluttering.
Giroie the Count de Montreuil there pight,
Whose praised name about the court did ring.
  He was so gentle and so fair a knight,
Who loved with Blanche, the fairest damozel
Of all who waited on our duchess bright.
  More shall ye learn of both: but now right well
That young and courteous knight remembered me,
And bore us company a little spell,
  And led us onward, gently talking he
To wild Diantha, till we gained the port
Of the fair lodging, decked with sylvan glee,
  Where young duke Richard held his summer court:
Who then with certain knights was set at board,
After the public hall, and all the sport.
  Never before saw I a mighty lord
Hold pleasant converse with his own compeers:
The doors were closed; the table was well-stored:
  No servitor appeared, but on three chairs
Sat by the duke the County of Ponthieu,
The Count of Brionne, the Count of Ferrières,
  Their banners over each: as in we drew,
More merry words heard we than wont to wag
Between high princes, so far as I knew.
  Ponthieu bade Brionne swallow his own flag,

And all began with laughing like to fall.
But I, who still about the door did lag,
  Beheld Sir Mano join those princes all;
Who made him right good cheer : then Mano gave
To the Duke's hand his letters special :
  And therewithal began discourse more grave,
And long time was maintained this interview.
These letters I with care collected have :
  And needful in this history to show
The evidence of what their scope and aim :
Since many of the things which here ensue,
  And Mano's expedition rose from them.

IV.—THE LETTERS OF COUNT THUROLDUS: OTHER LETTERS AND TIDINGS OF THE STATE OF THE WORLD.

" POPE Gregory our arms sanctificates:
    By virtue of which grace we have prevailed
As far as Bari and the Grecian gates.
  From Capua have we banished those who haled
Their cruel tribute to the apostate East,
And had destroyed them, but our forces failed :
  And now they gather strength again, increased
From Africa, Cyprus, and Sicily,
Whilst our late found advantage all is ceased.
  Much therefore it behoves that speedily
Succour ride forth from home : on thee it rests
To be our good in this necessity.
  Assist thou therefore unto these requests,
Most dread and sovereign lord, Gonnorides,
Despatching worthy aids : urge thy behests,

CANTO IV.]   A POETICAL HISTORY.

And move thy peaceful realm, as well agrees
Both with thy greatness and our exigence;
That future glory spring from present ease."
—— Of this epistle Mano made the sense
Ampler by various tidings that he brought,
And to our lords rehearsed in conference.

From him we learned what evils had been wrought
To Italy about that wretched time
By warring nations, which within her fought:
When Saracens held the whole Alps maritime,
And rode the seas beneath: Lombard and Greek
In combat ranged through fair Apulia's clime:
Nor yet the Norman power was main to wreak
Vengeance on those outrageous enemies,
The Norman power, now strong, that then was weak.

—— Moreover he to the East the Norman eyes
Was first to turn, and toward Jerusalem,
Where then our pilgrims met with injuries:
What time ruled there the negro Zacharem,
Who ravaged all the Holy Sepulchre,
Doing obedience to the race of Shem:—
He quenched the sacred light, which, all aver,
At Easter burns: and strove to obliterate
The cave where Joseph did the Lord inter.

Whereat a palmer, with high zeal elate
Smote with his fist the temples of a Jew,
Which deed for heinous crime the judge did rate;
And the Fatimite in raging fury slew
The man, and those who with him dared to stand,
Albeit to Italy escaped some few.

—All which our princes thought to take in hand,
And gathered closely in remembering mind,

Of the holy city and the eastern land.
—— But there were letters of more heavy kind,
Which rose beyond our mortal scope and bent,
Telling how wretched earth of heaven was pined.
   In them 'twas read how that poor land was rent
With troubles which no mortal might resist,
About that date when all the world seemed spent.
   Which revelation seemed of Antichrist,
Then sitting in God's temple, like to God;
Nor any sign of horror was there missed.
   " We feel," they wrote, " the sore avenging rod;
The famine and the unknown pest increase,
The secret fever which consumes the blood.
   " Men weakly wait, till death their pain bid cease,
The end their fellows little noticing,
Who for themselves desire the like release.
   " Their voices through the wasted fields of spring
Sound querulous, like to the dying birds
Which on the hard soil beat their helpless wing.
   " This plague invaded hath the flocks and herds,
The crops remained unsown this year; and now
What sustenance the naked field affords
   " They fight for till they die: it were as though
Confounded were the elements, and nature
Followed new laws: such anger clouds heaven's brow,
   " With tribulation of the whole creature:
For thrice the moon is marked with blood: the sun
Trembles to quit this circle of dark feature:
   " A mighty comet through the heavens doth run
Three months: discoloured are the stars by it:
Wherefore the last days seem to be begun.
   " —— This sign moreover doth St. John transmit,

That in the latter days we shall be tricked
By Satan's legates, men of subtle wit.
"And this last plague that holy men depict
Is added now: one such is hither borne,
Whose glozing style lies temper and inflict.
"Full many thousands have their faith forsworn
Through him, Vilgardus, named Grammaticus,
Who makes the Holy Church his mark of scorn;
"Fabling that on a summit mountainous
The demons of the poets came to him,
Juvenalis, Maro, and Horatius,
"Who hailed him their disciple, with no dim
Renown with them in realms beyond the grave,
And crowned him with a laurel garland trim.
"Then he of doctrine strange began to rave,
Uttering, 'twas thought, their oracles abhorred
Through the pretensed commission which they gave."
These were the tidings that were spread abroad
By writings, or the converse held in court
Betwixt Sir Mano and our gentle lord:
And deeply wrought they in the nobler sort.

V.—OF THE GREATNESS OF THE NORMANS.

THE Normans bear away the praise of might
From other nations in this age of war,
And raise their glorious name from height to height.
None other nation traverses so far;
And it might seem that numerous as the Dane,
Or Greek, or Saracen, the Normans are.
For never battle joins on any plain

Without some band of Normans in the brunt,
Whose sovereign arms the victory ordain :
  And through the seas the hidden isles they hunt
In shielded vessels, which those fleets of state,
That walk the orient waters, fear to affront.
  Nor only in the field they arbitrate
Between the nations : they as pilgrims go
To every shrine on earth by faith made great,
  Casino, Compostella, or the show
Of Tours, where all the relics may be found
That have been gathered in this age of woe.
  Yea, in the Holy Places they abound
Above all others : neither infidel,
Nor sea, nor desert, shuts the sacred ground :
  So that before their zeal invincible
The prospect of the world is open laid,
And they their lesson thence have learned full well.
  —— But if 'tis questioned, Whence be Normans made
Active above the others, who remain
Unmoving, darkened in ignoble shade,
  I answer, that religion breaks the chain
That sordid custom forges, and sets free
To nobler works from daily toil and pain.
  For other nations, chained upon the lea
In ceaseless labour, little guess or know
Beyond the feuds where they allotted be.
  In other nations the high seigneurs show
Seldom a spark, except in private war,
Of active conduct, or toward friend or foe :
  Each baron in his fort peculiar
Makes of his lands and people wasteful dearth,
And doth from common enterprise debar,

Maintaining bloody bands that drain the earth,
Like packs, their neighbours to devour and bite,
Not join with them in any deed of worth.
Thus France from blood and pillage hath respite
No single day : while all in peace abide
Through Normandy from duke to poorest knight.
No private war, no constant homicide
Distracts them ; but as if one family
They live in their domain from side to side.
So much in truth it profits them to be
The soldiers of the Church ; which is their boast :
And the high liegemen of the Holy See.
They go forth at her bidding as one host,
Plant where she wills their hardy colonies,
And when she leads the way, achieve the most.
But woe is me, that in this brave land lies
A cankerworm beneath the glorious show ;
Peace rests on pain, renown on miseries.
The peasants groan and wail in ceaseless woe,
Weighed down by tolls, by services and dues,
Which to their mighty lords they ever owe.
No task of them required may they refuse,
But, for themselves, to fish, or hunt, or snare,
Or fell the forest trees, they may not use :
Neither to spend upon themselves they dare ;
For all the Normans hold themselves to be
Equal as masters, having common care :
And hold the land by their confederacy,
Crushing the Frank and Breton, whom they found,
What time in ships they first came over sea.
 Which rigour wrought those children of the ground

To that mad rising, whose most sure defeat
Fell, ere the millenary year went round.
—— Well is it known, ere Richard took his seat
About that time, how under shade of night
The desperate foresters would ofttimes meet:
Until the Count of Evreux, Robert hight,
The Archbishop of Rouen, upon them fell
With a great following, by force and might.
That cruel lord broke their conventicle,
And pined them with torments in strange wise,
That dire examples might their courage quell.
Some he impaled, of some put out the eyes,
Of some he burned the members in quick lime,
And other nameless things did he devise.
The recollection of that hideous crime
I hold as parcel of the misery
Which I in convent suffered at the time.—
The bones that had been broken came to me
And to my piteous brethren, aching still
When all the fame thereof had ceased to be.
And slowly some we mended of their ill,
And pitied all; while question inly rose
Why some had right others to hold at will.—
"These poor men feel," methought, "as keen as those
Who so bestride them, nobles lithe and strong:
And yet bear those the whip, and these the blows.
"These have no place the lawgivers among,
But in their masters' eyes their statutes read
And must obey, smarting with bitter wrong.—
"Yet if to government they should succeed,
With wrongs would they redub the wrongs they felt,
Shake down the state, and furiously be freed.

"A bloody retribution would be dealt;
Mean vice would reign: then lands and holdings all
Into poor common portions they would melt.
"Then where were greatness, where were glory's call,
The arts, and whatsoever makes it good
That man exist beneath the fire-bright ball?"
And as to the abstract right, whether it stood
That few or many ruled, I could not tell;
But with the few still went the likelihood.
—— Thus with our minds discoursed we, at one spell
Tending poor wounds, and building up anon
By nobles' gifts our convent citadel:
And not much moved by us the world went on.

VI.—HOW DUKE RICHARD CAME TO FÉCHAMP.

THE leaves of the oak were falling on the ground
  When Richard read these letters: he decreed
That presently such succours should be found
  As Mano thought to meet the present need:
Who straight began his levies to collect.
Then his brave following back did Richard lead,
  And crossed the forest, that he might effect
A mournful penance at his father's tomb
At Féchamp, and a canonry erect:
  Richard, surnamed Gonnorides: than whom
No man more pious on the sun did look:
Sad piety constrained him thus to come.
  Nor shall I now omit to praise this duke,
Who was a prince of mild and gracious thought,

Holding his lofty state without rebuke.
  At Féchamp therefore passed we through the port
Into a pleasance fair and wide, wherein
Grew many trees around the sanded court:
 There fountains sprang, and runnels wandered clean:
And winding walks along rose-borders led:
And midst there was a goodly chantry seen,
 By the old duke before established,
And chambers, where with all her royal train
The duchess of young Richard had her sted:
 The sister of Duke Geoffrey of Bretagne
Was she, nor less in rank than beauty rare:
But fairest among all were ladies twain,
 And they were sisters ; namely, Blanche the Fair,
To whom Giroie was sworn, whom lately we
In Lyon forest found, when we passed there,
 And sweet Joanna, scarce less fair than she,
Joanna, for whose soul I bid you pray,
Sith ye shall sorrow for her history.
 And there I saw amid the others gay
That evil child Diantha also set,
Who wrought us all that trouble in the way.
  Now all the riders with sloped lances let
Their horses slowly pace these dames before:
And still the prayer-bell rang with clamour great:
 Then the duke entered by the chapel door,
And as he went, each footstep of the way,
The beadles strewed fresh rushes on the floor:
 Then down their staircase came those ladies gay.
On this side sat the duke, and upon that
Duke Geoffrey of Bretagne in like array.
 The ladies in their place appointed sat,

And all the knights came trailing two and two,
And ranged themselves on stool and bench and mat,
Mano, Brionne, Ferrieres, and Ponthieu.

VII.—HOW MANO CAST HIS LOVE AT BLANCHE: AND
HER SISTER AT HIM.

NOW in the chapel, ye shall understand,
   When sat those knights and ladies, gazing all
On one another, ranged on either hand,
   Ere that the chants began, it did befall
That Mano cast his eyes on Blanche the Fair;
   And of a bitter love became the thrall;
      Oh, bitterly love's thrall, Oh, then and there.
So that, although erewhile to Italy
He had been purposed swiftly to repair,
   His mind was changed, and he gan secretly
Devise to tarry longer in that place:
Which was his first fall from integrity.
         Nor less Joanna to her fate did race,
Who that same hour went into love as deep
With him, as he with Blanche. O cruel case!
   I, to whom mortal love is sin, can weep
At the most fatal stroke of love, which still
Of ordered joys makes but a tangled heap:
   When I consider all the bitter ill
Which came thereof: how Mano his life's peace
Lost in the mournful frenzy of his will:
   And how Joanna, till her soul's release,
Never knew joy, but hungrily did watch
The love which all so nigh her did increase:
   But, though so nigh, no glimmer could she catch,

Nor any ray of warmth : ah fate unkind,
That love's designs and deeds so ill should match !
　I say that I, though with a zealous mind
Devoted to the Benedictine rule,
Which blessed Odo on his monks did bind,
　And all my life instructed so to school
My senses to exclude love's very thought,
And turn from him who is love's slave and fool;
　Yet in my secret'st heart I never sought
To shut out pity for such misery;
So blessed Maiolus and Aylmer taught:
　They pitied too that human woe : and I
Who learned of them in youth, and still observed
Of those great men the grave austerity,
　Deem that in age I shall not thence have swerved,
If with full heart I write of what befell
Through love's great force : nay, thereto am I nerved,
　And in the thought of them think I do well :
Their reverend zeal and aspect so benign,
And their old age of toil within me dwell.
　When I and other youths, compeers of mine,
To evil thoughts gave way, and restless grew
Under the burden of our vows divine,
　Then Maiolus and Aylmer ever threw
Themselves between us and the gates of sin
With lifted hands and eyes of lovely hue :
　And their sweet counsel probed so deeply in
Our stormy hearts with loving words and wise,
That we with penitence would soon begin;
　Yea, break in tears, and strong tempestuous sighs,
And soon our feeble zeal was re-illumed
From their bright torch, with clearer flame to rise.

For they victorious emblems had assumed
Over the flesh, while we were fighting still:
They fly not fast whose souls for heaven be plumed:
But by God's law on earth they tarry till
Others grow strong who feebler pennons wave:
Nor did they this command austerely fill.
Oft in their dehortation mild they gave
Strange knowledge how in youth themselves were tried
By wiles from which themselves they could not save:
But if they stood, through grace it did betide:
And many a wondrous miracle they told
In which heaven's grace in them was magnified:
And many a penance undergone of old,
Through which their evil nature was subdued:
That we against the flesh might wax more bold.
    Then we ourselves in labours stern and rude,
Fasts, vigils, chantings, stripes, by slow degrees
Arose above each passion wild and lewd;
And as life passed, grew more and more at ease.
But life was well-nigh passed ere that, as now,
My mind her thoughts was able to appease,
And live by memory in times gone through,
And so collected as to gaze upon
The joys of others without present woe,
Their griefs without malignity thereon:
And even now at times I feel the wrong
Of having lived my woful life alone.
Why should I serve this toil? though I belong
Through this, I trust, to heaven's elected bands?
So feels the priest, when comes the nuptial throng,
Which day by day approaches where he stands
White-robed, awaiting, that they may partake

The holy marriage blessing from his hands.
No joy is stored for him, although he make
The joys of others holy, last of all
To be remembered, let him smile or ache.
Yet in this sadness it is usual
To find great peace : and only pity grows
In me beholding how men's woes befall.
But I will say, if ever aught arose
In me akin to thoughts which women move,
Joanna sweetest, sacred through her woes
To me—but what has that to do with love?

VIII.—OF THE CROSSES OF LOVE.

THOU poppy, that of Lethe art the flower,
 Why hangest thou down ere ripeness be begun,
Ere yet be come thy seasonable hour,
 That thou art lifted upward to the sun,
And bloomest high on thy erected stem,
Gazing the sky which late thou seemedst to shun?
 Thou wearest still thy scarlet anadem
While life remains : then downward fallest again,
More lifeless than when first thou wast a gem :
 And, ruined more and more by wintry rain,
Art gathered to thy root beneath the ground.—
So with man's heart, that shall of love be fain.
 It waits in rest ere yet it may be crowned
With love's fledge flower : then in maturity
With waving splendours fires the air around :
 Then enters on the day of misery,

The fickleness of time, the strokes of fate :
Love's stricken banners hover miserably,
　Life's rotting root in sadness lingers late,
Ere frozen age seal the sad residue,
And pottering death e'en that obliterate.
　　Of Mano I say this, that ne'er I knew
Aught like his love of Blanche : and this I say
Who have seen much that mighty love can do.
　All that befell I know : for in that day
He told me much, being familiar
To my society, while there we lay.
　For I had grown to love that knight of war,
So gracious was he to me, so would he
To me his fiery nature check and bar :
　And give me those kind looks which live in me,
Those lightsome words that warm like summer days,
But never rob the mind of dignity.
　And I to him was dear : nought shall efface
The recollection of those better hours,
Amid the deadly ills that I must trace :
　Which now began. His manner in those towers
Already feared me much : a reckless star
Seemed shaking over him malific powers.
　For friendship's sake I may not all declare,
Nor more than fits the story shall be shown :
But this in sum : he shunned the Italian war,
　And turning all his thoughts to Blanche alone,
Lost docile peace, and never more achieved
A quiet hour, but in love's net lay prone.
　The joy of Giroie him of joy bereaved,
Nor willed he to call home his chafed heart,
Ere all was lost too far to be retrieved.

Thus saw he fortune from his life depart:
But sadder still was poor Joanna's case,
Who bore in innocence love's bitter smart.
　For, many a day, as went the months apace,
They met, when he for Blanche her sister sought,
And she her own love banished from her face:
　So love herein contrariously wrought,
And this way fell it: Mano mightily
Loved Blanche, and of Joanna took no thought,
　But hoped himself to be loved answerably:
Which was not so, seeing that to Giroie,
That merry and good knight, betrothed was she:
　So that long time he fed upon false joy,
Deeming her easiness and happy cheer
Favour of him: so was he Fortune's toy.
　For all that time Sir Giroie came not near,
And Mano of Sir Giroie little knew,
Nor heard from others with a knowledge clear.
　But ye who shall this history pursue,
Shall find what strange adventure then befell
Giroie, which from the court his face withdrew,
　Whom we in Lyon forest deemed to dwell
In fair pavilion, as love's forester,
When he lay crouching close in horror's well.
　And touching Blanche, Mano no blame of her
Would ever grant, albeit she wrought him woe,
And cast him from her with disdainful cheer.
　He blamed himself, nor would he deign to owe
Comfort to blame of her: but still denied
That any friend on her reproach should throw;
　In truth, of love she never signified,
But long was he abused by everything

Which to the truth might best have been his guide:
And most Diantha imped his foolish wing:
For when that wicked one his case divined
She fed his hopes with vain imagining:
For to do harm best pleased her evil mind:
So that the wise was fooled. But at the last
Joanna, pitying his darkness blind,
Occasion took a light on him to cast,
And told him all the truth, how all things lay,
That Blanche the Fair and Giroie were trothfast.
    All that between them fell needs not to say;
But poor Joanna vainly hoped that he
Might shift his love to her from that same day;
    Alas not so: for in mild courtesy
He gathered what she of her sister said,
And, answered little, though moved verily.
    Nor she her sacred secret aught betrayed;
Nor guessed it he, even while his eyes were set
Upon the sweet face of that gentle maid.
    Why failed his thoughts to pierce the wan regret
Of love within that look?—'twas enough fair
To have touched one less enwrapped in other's net.
    Full lovely was the falling of her hair,
Sweet was her carriage, sweet the little folds
Of her fair dress close drawn with meekest care.
    Light as a bird she seemed in these dark holds
Of sin and woe, soft-footed as a dove:
No fairer soul the Mother's glance beholds,
    Since that she joined the virgin choir above,
And woe is ceased with her, and tears and sighs,
Which was the most she gained of earthly love.
    For Mano, hearing what she did avise,

Designed to go to Blanche, and there receive
The answer of these ambiguities,
  And otherwise no whit of all believe:
Which purpose was prevented many days;
In the which time this chanson did he weave.
  " Now my exalted heart plays with delays,
But soon may I wear victory's fair crown,
  And better celebrate my lady's praise,
  " When at her lovely feet my head goes down,
To lay one myrtle leaf on laurer wood.
Ah love ! My heart beats ; fiery sorrows drown
  " My eyes with dews of love, and in my blood
Is ice of shuddering mixed: my heart beats thick :
A din is in my ears : the pulses thud
  " Loud in my breast. Oh, gentle Love, come quick
Thy learning lay in every lingering line.
Teach, teach me all thy precious rhetoric,
  In praising her to praise thy power divine."

IX.—HOW BY BLANCHE SIR MANO WAS REFUSED AND
MADE FOOLISH.

SO was this strong man madly temperate,
  Until at last the evil day was come
For which so long cold Fortune bade him wait.
  And now that he and Blanche in closed room
Are met in converse, now 'twere not unmeet
That I should of the painter's skill presume.
  If ye would see that lady fair and sweet
In her first youth, she had wide flashing eyes,
And she was prompt of speech, and of some heat,
  Which ever to the proud gains enemies :

But, whom she had offended, she would be
Quick with some sudden kindness to surprise :
 And her great beauty made the amends as free
And acceptable as the smile of the air,
When from a cloud it looks more graciously.
 Well coloured was she, tall and debonair,
And light and very swift : and energy
And grace in all her actions mingled were.
 Her hair was long, her face made delicately,
Her lips and eyes were in a form so rare,
Which way she turned her neck, they did agree.
 And so she was surnamed Blanche the Fair,
And Rouen's Maid : seeing so fair she was
That not another might with her compare.

   To this fair creature Mano told his case
From the first day whereon his heart grew weak,
Beseeching her for gentleness and grace.
 But she anon bade him no more to speak,
Sith to Giroie her troth was given away
Long since, as all men knew. Red was her cheek ;
 Like a fool looked he : nought could he gainsay
But that of all the very truth he knew,
As sad Joanna told him ere that day.
 But now, he said, "Thou biddest me to rue :
Wisdom too late is folly's penalty :
Yet answer, for this one request I sue,
 "Thou who thus dealest forth my destiny,
That, knowing all, my fate the easier prove :
Goes this thing with thy mind?"—"Yea," answered she.
 "Then," answered he, "since love is born of love,
And thou returnest not my love for thee,
That which I brought must I again remove,

And in my breast must poor love buried be."—
"And even so, since never I thee bade
To vex me with thy love, I well agree:"
That answered Blanche: then without word he made
His passage from her presence fair and fierce;
And coming whence he was so evilly paid,
His beard was all to-rent beneath his ears.
But in a while he gan to smile, and sing
This little song, which in this place appears.
"I cry your mercy for my misdeeming:
An end of all my songs I make hereby:
For love hath made an end of his playing,
"And in love's joys no more a share have I.
And if of joy an end to me thou bring,
And thoughts of love within my mind must die,
Then of my songs there is no more to sing."

X.—HOW BOTH JOANNA AND MANO WOULD VISIT
GERBERT: AND HOW JOANNA MET AN OLD
PEASANT IN THE FOREST LAMENTING, WHO
TOLD HER HIS STORY.

NOW when Joanna saw what mien he wore,
And that of her no thought was in his mind,
Love's trouble in her bosom wrought so sore
That she lord Gerbert straight resolved to find
For counsel in her cause: and it befell
That Mano on his part the same designed.
The mighty Gerbert at that time did dwell
In Rouen not far off: thus sought they two,
Each unknown of the other, the same cell.

And first to say what things her journey through
Joanna met, who through the long woods went
Riding by glades and paths she little knew,
 Till the night fell, and she was somewhat spent
And terrified : then in a valley drear
She heard the voice of one who made lament :
 Which woful sound soon caused to disappear·
From her mild bosom dreariness and dread :
And to the place she turned and drew anear.
 There in the darkness at the valley's head,
An aged peasant sat and made his moan :
Who to her asking thus the occasion said :
 " I to my neighbour give this mournful groan,
And to his wife, and the great wickedness
Of my own daughter, which shall now be known.
 My neighbour, to his own unhappiness,
Above all things desired his son to be
Married to her whom mine I must confess,
 And to the same full well did I agree :
For our two farms were in this valley lone,
Where they were nurtured in their infancy,
 In childhood played together, and being grown
Were in each other ordered to confide.
But from the first froward my child was known ;
 True love might never in her soul abide :
And in the place of gentle intimacy
They did but ever wrangle, scoff, and chide.
 So that if love at first moved actively
Within my neighbour's son, yet soon it died.
But now, the more it seemed unlike to be
 That he should take my daughter for a bride,
The more his father would that so he should,

And fixed his mind upon no thought beside.
  And one day walking in this mountain wood, '
Casting this case full sadly in his mind,
He met the evil wight in the peaked hood,
  Who told him how by art he had divined
His trouble, and that he should yet ere long
His son in marriage with my daughter bind.
  This comfort made his hope again wax strong :
But time went on, and love increased no whit
In that injurious pair, but pride and wrong.
  They would not in one room together sit,
Nor lead their flocks nor cattle the same way,
Nor space for thought of peace did they permit.
  For if upon the hill her flock did stray,
He in the valley kept : if she the vale,
He held the hill through all the summer day.
  So that our hopes again began to pale.
And therewithal did damage great ensue
To our poor stock : both houses like to fail :
  For we instead of one were now made two
By this perversity : and at the last
I sought my neighbour's wishes to subdue,
  And thus I urged him. 'Neighbour, now is past,'
Said I, 'the term these follies to allow :
Give up the thought on which thy mind is placed.
  'For neither of them to our wishes bow,
And we are sundered by their enmities.
Therefore thy son away from this send thou,
  'And we in both our houses shall have peace.
[Nay, otherwise we cannot live, nor draw
Subsistence from these miserable leas :]
  'Persuaded be thou therefore.' But I saw

Great sorrow take him at my words, and so
I did the matter for the time withdraw:
And he spake of the things he wished the mo."

XI.—THE PEASANT CONTINUES HIS STORY.

WHEN that poor peasant to this point was come,
    He stayed and sighed: " Ah, wherefore wishes vain
Make in the breast of wretched men their home,
    And most concerning children: who with pain
Being born, and nurtured in their infancy,
Still, after nonage past, a care remain;
    Nor can we parents, to our misery,
The former manage of their state forbear,
Or free our hearts from old anxiety.
    For how to shape their course is still a care,
Neither may we reject and cast away
Our fullgrown offspring anyhow to fare,
    As do the beasts, their hearts to disarray
Of tenderness, when infant cries are o'er;
Alas, we toil and spin till we be grey!
    —My hapless neighbour, who still hoped the more
That every day he saw his hopes decline,
Ended them all in sudden trouble sore,
    When went his son one day to herd the swine
In yon oak forests whence the vale is sought,
And ne'er again returned, and left no sign.
    In vain his parents Heaven for him besought,
They never knew what I too well can say—
That in the woods, far from his father's cot,
    He met the evil wight who doth waylay
The dwellers hereabout; and being prone

To mischief, did his evil hests obey:
   And so on him by art a charm was thrown
To make him seem another: by which spell
Disordered, in the woods he journeyed on,
   Till in the company of thieves he fell,
As it was like to be: he met a band
Of pillers, and agreed with them to dwell,
   And soon was known chief robber in the land,
By name of Riculf: and, to crown this height,
That gang so bold their practice took in hand,
   That they assailed the castle of a knight,
And slew him, and in prison cast his son.
And thence, so dealt the evil valley-wight,
   This knave a guise so like the son put on,
That he usurped his name, (his own real state,
Save to his comrades, being known to none):
   And him he pined, whom he did personate,
With pining sore, and kept in prison strong,
And in foul living wasted his estate.
   "Some time being passed these wicked deeds among,
There fell on this foul cheat a sickly blight:
He took to bed, he wasted, and ere long
   The spreading pain deprived his eyes of sight.
Whereat he bade proclaim a great reward
To any who should bring him back to light.
   Then many famous surgeons, when they heard,
And many other wanderers, him to please,
The journey to the dangerous manor dared:
   They brought strange drugs to give him sight and ease,
But when each failed, the most remorseless brute.

Who lay in bed, wrung dreadful penalties :
For from their heads the living eyes he cut,
And sent them groaning o'er the drawbridge steep:
So perished they who dared this vain pursuit.
Thenceforth none ventured to approach his keep:
And with the fell disease which racked his frame
The wretch was left alone, to wake or sleep.
 " At length, after some days, a young man came,
Asking to put a medicine to the test,
That he might do the cure and win a name.
Then e'en those thieves to whom he made request,
So brave he seemed, were sorry in good sooth
To see him run on danger manifest:
And fain would have withheld him, but the youth
Prevailed to have his way; and so was brought
Unto the bed of that blind man uncouth :
Who warned him of the torment to be wrought,
If his nigh hopeless hope were unfulfilled;
But the youth smiled, as not regarding aught,
And presently upon his eyes distilled
A wondrous liquid, which at once made clear
Their glaring round, which rage with blood had filled.
Their light returned to them, and from their drear
And horrid stare moving, they first beheld
The keen smile of that youth so close and near:
Who with his phial, bent like one impelled
By waking first to scan his bed-fellow
Still sleeping; nor long time his smile withheld :
But, as he gazed, broke into laughter low
To see him seeing, and himself be seen :
And tossing down his phial said, ' Lo, lo !
What wonders I can work, if that I mean !'

The other leaped from bed : 'Brave youth,' said he,
'Ask anything thou wilt; command me e'en
　To the thousandth of my little territory.'
But the youth laughed again : said he, 'I crave
Not to command thee for my doctor's fee,
　But rather to obey thee as thy slave.'
And therewithal her bosom bare she laid,
Drawing her robe apart; then stared the knave,
　For he was talking with a lovely maid.
Wherewith full soon o'erjoyed to her he ran,
But she with graceful hand did him evade :
　'Nay, fear,' said she, 'thine own physician !
Full oft of old have I thy form admired,
Begirt with many a gallant serving-man,
　When in our vale thy glittering hunts have fired
The forest woods : full often have I prayed
That heaven would raise me to thy height desired ;
　For I was lowly born, by fate betrayed,
And by my parents kindlessly designed
To marry one whom fate my equal made ;
　One, as in station low, so base in mind,
A wretched swineherd's son, a sordid pest,
A hideous and miserable hind :
　But my disgust with hate soon filled his breast,
And some few months ago he disappeared,
And left the valleys and the hills at rest.'
　—"'Well,' quoth the knave, when this account he
　　　heard,
And knew my daughter, whom he hated erst,
As now he loved with fury, being assured
　She knew him not in his disguise accursed,
'Go on, thou lovely stranger, tell to me

What blessing told thee of my sickness first?'
—"'I saw the hunt one daybreak,' answered she,
'In joyous summer riding round the wood,
And thou wast not among their company.
Then mournful in my flock long time I stood,
Ere at my side I saw an aged wight,
Who told me thou wast playing blind-man's hood
  Against thy will; then pensive with the night
Homeward I fared; and sat full sad and still,
Until my angry mother gan me smite,
  And chide me for high thoughts and wayward will;
And bade me next our supper to prepare:
And when I scorned to mix the wretched swill,
  She called the swineherd, him whose noble heir
I was to wed, to force me to obey:
The ready refuge of her sordid care.
  To him she raced, my father being away,
And he came quickly with his fingers spread,
And dragged me to his hut, which thereby lay:
  Where to his wife me he delivered,
"Upon this wicked disobedient trull
Revenge thou thy son's loss," to her he said.
  The eyes of that old wife, of fury full,
Sparkled when she beheld me; and full soon
My long hair loose with curses did she pull,
  And beat me sore, and haled me up and down;
Nor from her cruelties desisted she,
Till to the ground I staggered in a swoon.
  "This story mixed of spiteful falsity
My wicked daughter gave, as I received
From one who in the place happened to be.
  But now the knave who heard, and well believed

D

What his own thoughts desired, bellowed on high,
' By Satan, they who thy fair head mischieved
   Of such a deed the cost shall well aby,
Though they my father and my mother were.'
Then she, ' Let me tell on their cruelty.
   ' Next morning did these swineherds reappear,
Leaving the wretched chamber where they lay,
And offered me to share their meagre cheer.
   ' Then, when their summons I would not obey,
Shut in the house was I till eventide,
And slept that night upon the floor of clay.
   ' The next day was the same on either side :
But on the third, when the man took his road,
Against the watchful wife my strength I tried,
   ' And quickly left that villainous abode.
Nor hied I home ; but up the valley went,
Where soon I marked that one before me strode :
   ' Who, keeping still before, his footsteps bent
Into the glades of the wide-spreading wood,
Then turned and waited me :—" Oh, excellent,"
   ' Said he ; " thou pupil spirited and good,
Save that thou long hast kept me waiting here."
Him then the same old carle I understood,
   ' Who haunteth ever in the valley drear,
Who told me of thine ill ; he told me now
How all thy surgeons thou hadst quitted dear :
   ' But bade me, armed with this strong philtre, go,
Fearless, and pour the liquor in thine eyes.
Thou knowest the rest ; deserve I thanks or no ? '
         " Then the knave kissed her ; and to win his
            prize
That very night he sent a numerous band

Of his own servitors in sure disguise
  To my poor neighbour's cot with this command,
Him and his aged wife to bring away :
That is, his parents, thou mayst understand.
  Alas for them ! for in the night heard they
A fiendish yelling round their little place ;
And looking out saw it as light as day,
  With torches burning in their garden space,
And the False Faces in disorderly
And frightful dresses, with great headpieces.
  Then, in their dreadful misery, to fly
In darkness to the woods that wretched pair
Thought first; and might have saved themselves thereby.
  But at that moment from the outer air
Sounded a solemn voice, ' Go, fearing nought,
If ye would see your son married to her,
  The woman whom to be his bride ye sought.'—
And the poor father knew the valley-wight,
Who erewhile to his ears that promise brought.
  And they surrendered to his evil might,
And with that company they went along,
Suffering hard usage through the weary night ;
  And saw so many spectacles of wrong
Upon the way, that they were well-nigh dead
Ere they arrived before the castle strong.
  There, lifting up with pain each aged head,
They saw indeed their son, that felon high,
And my vile child, by him dishonoured.
  And on them in that house of villainy
The voices thick of fiends began to shower
Insult and taunt and all impiety.
  And thus these parents gained a child the more ;

Thus their life's fondest wishes did they gain,
Thus they their son recovered in that hour.
   The magic hid him not; they saw him plain,
And speechless fell in death in that ill place.
And this is that with sorrow I complain :
My wicked daughter, and their evil case."

XII. — HOW JOANNA FARED ONWARD WITH THE
    PEASANT : AND HOW SIR MANO MET WITH A
    WOUNDED MAN.

NOW when Joanna heard that doleful tale,
   Soft pity filled her: and she minded then
To be in misery of some avail.
   Therefore she bade the cottage-denizen
To lead her to that home of cruelty,
Nor feared alone to visit such foul den.
   Right glad the peasant was: forth did they hie,
And sought it through the woods a weary stage;
So in the long woods leave we them thereby.
       For now, too, love in quest of Gerbert sage
Hath sent Sir Mano forth : and straight rode he
Along the river in such pilgrimage.
   When casting round his eye he chanced to see
A man, who lay as dead in the green shaw :
To whom speaking, groans him answered grievously.
   Then riding near, the wretch's eyes he saw
Wrapped in a bandage poor, bedrenched with gore;
And bitter torments seemed his limbs to draw;
   For his white face turned toward the heaven he bore,
Shuddering and moaning still. "What man art thou,"
Said Mano, " dying in this weather frore,

CANTO XII.] A POETICAL HISTORY. 37

"That mid the battering leaves dost mope and mow?"
—"Cold is this place, and bitter is the ache
Of ceaseless pain," the other answered slow,
"But well it is, if thou darest vengeance take
On evil doer, that I nursed my breath
To speak the wrongs which me thus wretched make."
  Then Mano raised the man, who seemed nigh death,
And comforted him all that there he could:
And presently with pain the other saith:
"Behold this napkin stiff with oozing blood:
It hides the sightless circles of mine eyes,
Which never more shall look on ill or good:
They only feel, not see, their miseries,
Themselves a sight most piteous, seeing nought,
Though of my sorrows faithful witnesses.
  I was a surgeon once, and wisely taught,
Save that I trusted in my art too well:
For too much confidence me hither brought.
  Southward from hence a castellan doth dwell,
And many miles is spread his wide domain:
On whom erewhile a foul disease there fell,
  Which in dark scales his eyelids still doth chain;
As thou art knight of gentle courtesy,
On him, beseech thee, wreak my wrongs amain.
  For from that caitiff's heart of cruelty
This custom vile against them was begun
Who should their art to him in vain apply,
  That they should for ill surgery atone
By loss of their own eyes:—full many tried
The dangerous venture: and I, wretched one,
  Who on a mighty medicine relied,
Likewise in turn to do him good essayed,

Alas, in vain : me did that fiend deride,
 Gladder that I was vanquished in my trade
Than sorry for his eyesight unrestored :
And thence he bade me be to doom conveyed.
 His ministers with point of piercing sword
Put out my light for ever, and so left
To grope my dark way from their felon lord.
 The loss of eyes of living me bereft :
Cold, darkness, wandering, and weariness
And hunger unappeased my being cleft:
 Cast was death's shuttle through my mind's distress ;
Down, down, I fell ; and dying here I lie."
Then said Sir Mano, " By death's holiness,
 " These wrongs upon that felon wreak will I,
If he be named."—" Giroie de Montreuil,"
The other said, and Mano made reply,
 " To hear that name a double spur I feel,
Since scarcely he my friend : yet is he told
A better knight than thou dost him reveal,
 " And in his actions gentle, just, and bold."
Then said the other, " Death is here ; I give
To thee a guerdon in this ring of gold,
 " And bid thee keep it safe while thou shalt live :
It bears a poison of such quality,
That whoso in his mouth the same receive,
 " In that same moment of earth's ills is free :
To use it on myself was in my mind ;
Think I am grateful if I give it thee."
  Then that man's soul with pain did death unbind,
And Mano felt great pity to behold,
And in its garments did the poor corpse wind,
 Composed it decently, and in the mould

Dug, as he could, a grave, the same to hide
From wolf or lynx, and great logs thither rolled,
  And beat them in with earth on every side,
And set a brushwood fence both thick and high
All round, the which atop with twigs he tied,
  Using a fallen tree that lay thereby;
And over all he laid great boughs across;
And after labour long, he forth did hie,
To find the man who caused this harm and loss.

XIII.—HOW MANO MET WITH GIROIE.

LONG held he onward till he reached the ground
  Whereon that manor stood, which stood full high,
And was on every part inclosed around.
  So that he lingered in the wood hard by,
Thinking to mark the passages, ere yet
Unto the gate itself he came anigh.
  When in an alley thick with trees inset
Presently he beheld riding a knight,
Whom above all 'twas welcome to have met.
  For from his shield, which bare device full bright
He seemed to be Giroie: then Mano cried,
" Thou wicked caitiff, if thou have thy sight,
  " Which to restore full many a man hath died,
To keep thee from me thou shalt have ado,
And need to use thy eyes on every side."
  And therewithal full fiercely they fell to:
But Mano, when he found what way came on
That feigning semblance, to great wonder grew:
  For scarcely gave he stroke, and stood to none,
Nor bore his shield on high in knightly sort,

When the strait place gave sore occasion:
But twisted in his seat, with knees drawn short:
And uttered gibes when strokes went nigh his head;
So that with wrath his very horse gan snort.
But not for ever could such game be played,
And in short time Sir Mano with great might
Upon the ground that senseless felon laid.
Whom minding to have slain for felon knight,
And rashing off his helm thereto, he found
Another man in Giroie's armour dight.
Then, as he thought thereon, the windy round
Of the forest seemed to whisper : and behold,
Joanna, and the peasant in that sound!
Full soon'that fallen man the peasant old
Knew for the knave who owed so much of blame,
And therewith bade the knight his hand withhold,
Since better he deserved a death of shame
Than to be nobly slain by gentle hand.
—Then well Sir Mano greeted that fair dame,
Who for his sake was journeying through the land,
Albeit he knew it not: but now anon
The peasant's tale they made him understand:
And forward to the castle set they on,
Which that false knave usurped, who now was tied
Securely in the midst, his horse upon.
But when his lusty quean their coming spied,
She made the gates all fast, and on the wall
Lay watching : unto whom her father cried,
"Thou wicked offspring of hell's bitter gall,
Know thy ill deeds discovered, and thy knave
Taken, and now at hand thy fatal fall.
" If there within be any good and brave,

Open the gates, I say! and help to wreak
On her of many men the bloody grave;
" And on this quaking wretch, who cannot speak,
Revenge the heir, who is in prison pined
By this false caitiff here for many a week."
  When thus he spoke, like to a rising wind
There rose a noise within : and presently
Shouts, blows, and groans, a hubbub fell and blind.
 Against the thieves who there did occupy
Many now sided, who liked not that sin,
And had been murmuring long in secrecy.
 Then, when grew loud the fighting and the din,
Sir Mano blew his horn with mighty sound,
Whereat the gates flew open from within;
 And in he hurled, and dealt such strokes around,
That in short time the victory was won,
And all the robbers who yet lived were bound.
 Then went they to the prison, where the son
Of the old lord was laid in bondage strong,
Whom out they drew with famine all foredone.
 Thin was his body, and his hair grown long,
Enwrapped was he in rags, shaking with cold;
But round his neck her arms Joanna flung.
 Which when Sir Mano saw, and gan behold
The lover of the lady whom he loved,
Namely the true Giroie, that knight full bold,
 A little smiled he, and himself removed,
And stood apart a little at the sight.
Then to him came Giroie, as him behoved,
 And gave him thanks for rescue done in fight :
For well he knew what should to worth belong,
Nor lived a kinder man in earthly light :

He then, unknowing of love's bitter wrong,
To Mano rendered thanks with countenance bright,
And him Sir Mano answered with this song :—
    " Doing myself wrong, fought I for the right,
I with no quarrel drew my heavy blade,
And in advantage placed my opposite.
    " Out of a foe a deadlier friend I made,
A castle took I for the castellan,
Restoring him who yet therein was laid.
    " For my own love freed I another man,
And 'gainst myself to fit him paid my blood ;
By my own victory my defeat began.
    " And by this sequel it is understood
Wherefore these many weeks before this day
This knight before my lady hath not stood.
    " For he in prison strong forpined lay,
The while that I from her dismission gained :
But now may Christ hearken to that I say—
    " Albeit I by her am thus disdained,
No force nor might of any man shall stay,
And against all it is by me maintained,
    " That she be lady of my thoughts alway,
Both day and night to rule within my breast,
And that I do her service if I may."
    Then sighed Joanna, hearing him protest
To have what fate was settled to deny :
For in her hopes that storm was laid at rest.
    But now Giroie to Mano made reply
With eyes surprised, but yet of courteous cheer,
Saying, " If thou love her whom no less I,
    " There lies no cause of wrath or hate or fear ;
For, if I might all things declare to thee,

Thou shouldst not deem my part so poor in her,
" Nor think that envy so should work in me,
That I should grudge thy thoughts their happiness."
Then Mano briefly answered, " It may be."
　　　But now to punishment they gan address
Their thoughts for those ill doers who remained,
The knave and his fair leman in distress,
　　　Who still their former countenance maintained,
And in the midst being brought, the knave all pale
And streaked with blood, and both of them enchained ;
　　　Of whose fell crimes when witness did not fail,
Sir Mano said, " To mercy is my mind,
And, as my sword to win them did prevail,
　　　" So to their father be my right resigned,
And be that sentence given that he avise."
For to his own he deemed he would be kind.
　　　But that old man arose with heavy sighs,
And in the midst his sentence gave anon,
Which came on all who heard with full surprise.
　　　" Daughter," said he, " and by ill chance my son,
Full deeply have ye sinned, and trespass tried
Which few that are worst sinners would not shun ;
　　　" Slaying your parents : but if now beside
Your murdered parents none for vengeance call,
Then I forgive you, speaking on the side
　　　" Of those poor parents ; yea, forgive you all
That their grave covers, well assured that they
Would bid no spot of harm on you to fall.
　　　" But others were there in your evil day
Whom one of you with cruel torment slew,
And for false deeds besides your lives must pay.
　　　" O children, I your father pass on you

This righteous judgment, That upon yon wall,
Within whose bound ye earned your evil due,
   " Ye both be hanged on high, and so end all—
This only is it that I may decree,
Nor from just mouth may other sentence fall.
   " Though anguish weigh me down and misery,
Yet know I, and yourselves must own, the right,
Nor part from me in anger—woe is me ! "
            Thus saying went he to the youthful wight,
And spake with him full long; and at the last
The young man wept, and owned the sentence light,
   To die but once for all his vileness past.
Then to his daughter likewise did he go ;
But she, like a caught adder, stood aghast,
   Stiffened with rage, and would not once allow
That he should touch her ; so in anguish drear
That father turned away to hide his woe.
   Anon the ministers of death drew near,
And to the rampart high took they the road,
And met their death in sight of all men there.
   But first of all from out that ill abode
With stricken heart the peasant father fled :
And from the rampart each to other showed
   Long time his low-bent form, and hanging head.

XIV.—HOW MANO AND JOANNA CONTINUED THEIR
             JOURNEY.

IF thou canst tell why the root downward grows
   And the stalk upward, thou mayst also say
Why one is born to joys and one to woes,
   One sinks, one rises, in the self-same day :

And above all why fickle love doth rate
Fortune against man's merit in his play:
  To one man rendering joy and solace great,
To others like worth cause to sigh and groan,
Life's lure to this, to that the fist of fate.
      Lo now the case of Mano and of Joan.
They both of worth deserved love's bliss to mede,
And yet of him had only dule alone.
  Forth from that evil house gin they proceed,
And none are very nigh them on the road:
Now is love's hour, methinks, for some kind deed.
  Now upon Mano love should lay his load,
Sith well that lord of all, that destiny,
Knew that her thoughts to Mano only flowed.
  Ah, none deserved love's answer more than she:
A scarlet hood with darker crossings held
Her tender face, that looked but wan of ble,
  As if she must have wept, but still withheld:
For in her mind what Mano lately said
Still tired her thoughts, and her sweet hopes dispelled;
  And though on Blanche his love was wholly laid,
Yet certainly, when Mano saw her now
Riding beside him in the forest shade,
  To her fair beauty all his mind did bow;
As the other deemed he her almost as fair,
And saw the other in her lovely brow;
  For much her face did that resemblance wear,
And in her voice her sister's voice awoke.
Neither could he his longing oft forbear,
  But touched her gentle forehead, or would stroke
Her hand that kept the rein; which she allowed.
Ah, could he but have rent shame's unfast cloak,

And seen her heart, which love left little proud,
Her heart, which scarcely lay from him concealed,
And trembled still within its trembling shroud.
  But at the last upon the banked field
They sat together down : there did they kiss :
And much they trembled both ; but unrevealed
  Joanna kept herself in troubled bliss.
She trembled unto shuddering : he the same :
But neither of them said one word, I wis.
  Yet kissed they one another without shame.
Lips travelled over cheek and mouth by turn
For a long hour : at least this blessing came
  On their unhappiness : this sweet sojourn :
Thus at the first at least did they embrace :
But what their last embracement ye shall learn.
  Ah, had he been content with that sweet face !
But even in the midst of that delight
Thought of the other in his mind had place,
  And made him feel ashamed and void of right
To hold a virgin soul so freely given :
Disturbed was he by love's tyrannic might,
  Nor kept the haven whither he was driven :
For words should have succeeded, and sweet vows,
Bearing them witness in the sight of heaven.
  She would have answered underneath the boughs,
And whispered him of love with sweetest breath :
Instead of that he must her mind arouse,
  And call himself to life almost through death,
And e'en for love love's perfect taste forego.
" The skies grow dark, the hour is late," he saith :
  And by a shamed smile to her doth shew
That all was nought.   Alas ! what case was this ?

To kiss and not be loved—with her 'twas so.
To kiss and not to love—that lot was his.
  Thence shamefast, no more hand in hand they ride:
And, knowing now the more their miseries,
End their dark journey in night's midmost tide.

XV.—CONCERNING GERBERT.

BUT now concerning Gerbert I shall write,
  To whom came these unhappy, seeking aid,
As men in darkness move toward the light,
  Each knowing not the other so arrayed.
Of Gerbert then I speak : he was the man
Who rose the highest in that age of dread.
  First in Aurillac he a monk began :
Whence being expelled, he to Cordova went,
  And thence reputed a magician :
For many years among the Moors he spent,
Learning astrology and alchemy,
Ere that to Rome his wandering feet were bent :
  Where, having made a wondrous clockwork, he
Gained commendation to the Emperor,
And tutor to his son advanced to be.
  Then to king Robert was he preceptor :
Master in Rheims of the cathedral school,
And then archbishop there, what time they bore
  The good archbishop Arnulph from his rule
By unjust might, till Rome stopped Gerbert's reign,
Sending a legate with peremptory bull :
  Whereon good Arnulph took his seat again,
And Gerbert wandered up and down the land
Full of fierce wrath, and burning with disdain :

The pope contemned he, and held no command
In the Lord's army, till within a while
Again great Otho took him by the hand.

Then was he lifted to his former style,
Archbishop of Ravenna he became,
And in new covert found new force and guile.

Forth from Ravenna's fort he levelled aim
Against the popedom, boasting to maintain
The freedom Gallican against that claim.

But here to my intent it is not main
In that concern to show him right or wrong,
But only his strange story to explain:

Which was divided thus: to be for long
The enemy of Rome; then, being made pope,
Beyond all former Fathers stout and strong;

The same that spread the Roman name and scope
Furthest abroad, was he at first who dared
The boldest pull against the Roman rope.

But he the same in all things still appeared,
Great, crafty, haughty.—Many men of fame
Unto God's service in his school were reared:

As Remi of Auxerre, whom others name
Haimon the Wise, who wrote upon the Mass;
Hubold, who did the blessed office frame

Which has the title Sancta Trinitas,
And many hymns: the good Leotheric
Of Sens archbishop: and of such I was:

I, who beheld how grave and politic
Was Gerbert with them, who yet honoured me
With singular care and apprehension quick.

Perchance in me he thought with certainty
To find a vessel of obedience;

CANTO XV.]   A POETICAL HISTORY.

And, but for fate, this had been verily.
But Mano's case in me made difference,
And love of Mano in those days began
To put down Gerbert from chief eminence.
 They call lord Gerbert a magician;
But if some stories I shall here repeat—
Part of the attendant fame that round him ran—
 They prove but only that the man was great,
And held high powers around him by his skill,
Not that they came through diabolic feat.
 Howso these stories, if incredible,
Or admirable only, I set down
Concerning him: accept them whoso will.
 For it is said that in the Roman town
A brazen statue stood with outstretched arm
Bearing the word "Dig here:" great this renown,
 And many they who dug and came to harm,
Not finding aught, nor guessing what was meant,
Till Gerbert reached it by a magic charm.
 He marked what way the hand its shadow bent
Upon the equinox and at the noon,
Then dug, and found much gold, but sore was shent:
 For a brass demon, keeper of the boon,
Leaped on him, and he scarce departed thence,
Leaving the riches o'er the cavern strewn.
 Again 'tis rumoured that in conference
The devil told him that Jerusalem
Should see his death: whereas he parted hence
 In the Church of Holy Cross, a stratagem
Being played on him, that church being oft so named:—
But that in death the fiend he did contemn:
 For ere his death his corpse was torn and maimed

E

By the Evil One, but yet with his last breath
He gave advice how Satan might be shamed :
 For in a cart to lay him after death,
And bury where the horses stopped, he bade :
And they unchecked, e'en as the story saith,
 Stopped at the Lateran, where he is laid :
And from the clatter of his bones, the sweat
And moisture of his marble, it is said,
 Omens and warnings to this day they get
When any pope may be about to die :
These and more doubtful things they tell ; which yet
'Tis better to relate than to deny.

XVI. — HOW BOTH JOANNA AND MANO CAME TO
GERBERT : AND WHAT FOLLOWED.

AT that time Gerbert was upon the track
 Of his advancement to Ravenna's see ;
And much he sought for instruments to back
 In every way his widespread policy :
For he abroad capacious nets had laid,
 And held in thought e'en now the papacy.
 But they who seek from others to have aid
The higher that they rise, the scarcer find
Men to fulfil their great requirements made.
 He therefore, having Otho well inclined
(Who had upraised him) for his furtherance,
Had fixed on Mano in his secret mind,
 Knowing the valour of the Norman lance,
And the knight's fame in war, deeming that he
Above all else his projects might advance.
 Wherefore to his return to Italy

He looked with hope, that he might be the plough
To break the rigid powers from sea to sea,
 That Greek and Saracen to him might bow,
Spreading his even power along the land,
And rival counts and dukes his head allow.
 These arts lord Gerbert well might understand,
Who held the whole world under scrutiny,
And upon every engine laid his hand.
 He now in Rouen in much privacy
With Robert the archbishop there conversed
Concerning matters of necessity;
 That Robert 'twas, whom Robert the accursed
I name; for to the heart in sordid greed,
To the lips was he in luxury immersed,
 And overhead in blood and cruel deed,
Though Richard's brother; whom in truth to be
The better churchman nature had decreed.
     Much marvelled Gerbert, when his face to see
A damsel craved, and asked his ear alone;
And lo! Joanna entered presently:
 Who told him of her love to Mano flown,
Of her great sorrow, of her travel sore,
And that her love was to the knight unknown.
 Then Mano's love to Blanche she set before
His questioning gaze; and how the more to gain
Her mind he strove, he was but mocked the more:
 And told him (but the telling was in vain
Since this he knew) that Blanche loved but Giroie,
And trothfast being to him, would so remain.
 —" Receive thou then what bitterest annoy,
What bitterest annoy and ceaseless pain
Hath ravaged and made boot on peace and joy.

"Mark what compulsion doth my soul constrain,
Against the modesty which maidens owe,
To break reserve, and unto thee complain."

Then Gerbert said, "Sweet daughter, even so
As a sick dove flies from her pined nest,
And nestles to her master in her woe,

"So comest thou to me, by love distressed :—
But that same dove, being hurt unto the death,
Would never seek to any human breast;

"She in her cote would breathe her failing breath,
And in like manner, if thou seek to me,
Bitter, but yet not mortal is thy scaith.

"I think, if I shall thy physician be,
That scorn to have been scorned, as I divine,
In man's proud mind with love doth ill agree :

"And this with Mano worketh to decline
New proffered love, though sweet and gentle thou :
He for his foredone love will rather pine."

But she returned, "Nay, thou mayst tell him now
That for Giroie if Blanche have him denied,
Love of Giroie I once did disallow,

"And sent him filled with anger from my side,
When first on me his thoughts were rather turned,
Than on the fairer one, when both he eyed."—

"Then equal stand ye," said he, "spurned for spurned :"
He smiled, "and that may comfort Mano's heart.
Daughter, thy tender shrift success hath earned.

"For if with him be wanting but my part,
With him shall I deal gravely in this case,
Sith worthy of my careful mind thou art.

"But now I bid thee hence to speed thy chase,
Unto a house which well is known to me,

Yclept Beyond Four Rivers : a fair place :
" There for the nonce shalt thou in safety be,
And I shall give thee letters unto those
Who there abide in closest nunnery :
" And likewise this, which thou shalt not unclose
(So secret is the thing) before the day
That thou shalt hear me done with mortal woes,
" Or that I bid thee break the seal away.
Which whensoe'er it happen, thou shalt know
That I of kindness made no vain delay."
    This said he : and Joanna thanks to owe
Not doubting, and in mind much comforted,
Forth from the palace on new quest did go.
    But scarcely thence her timid steps were sped,
When Mano in his turn to Gerbert came,
And told the love that he still cherished,
 And all of Blanche, that fair denying dame.
Which Gerbert hearing was in doubtful mind
To show or hide Joanna's trembling flame.
 But, casting much about, at last did find
That it were better now the same to hide,
Because of those great deeds which he designed :
 Lest Mano should from fame be turned aside.
Wherefore he kept the thing in secrecy,
And with Sir Mano now began to chide :
 Why on one woman still his mind should be,
When there were many in the world as fair :
And with long speech he gave love's history :—
 How many hopeful men had known despair,
And wasted all for love : how waymenting
Came in joy's place, and sorrow and dark care,
 When Love on wretches made his harrying.

All which moved Mano nought, and from his heart
Lightened the inner raging not a thing.
 "Whereat the other, " Of love's poisoned dart
I see the deadly working, O my son ;
Yea, fatal love possesseth every part :
"The dreadful power that mortal natures own,
The infection of the world! Yet not the less
Shall I expel the tyrant from his throne,
 " If not by reason, then by strange distress.
For know thou that the hour which now is night
(As each day's orb doth twelve twin hours compress),
"This hour, weeks gone, beheld in sunny light
Blanche and Giroie before the altar stand,
And I was priest to do the marriage rite :
" I joined the knight and lady hand in hand.
Wherefore behold, too late I find thee here
Entangled thus in love's constraining band."
 Then Mano said, " To whom for counsel clear
I looked midst all, that man to me hath shown
The thirling point of Fortune's fatal spear,
And by her hand upon it lays his own."

XVII.—GERBERT TELLS SOMETHING OF MANO'S BEGINNINGS.

THOU only bird that singest as thou flyest,
 Heaven-mounting lark, that measurest with thy wing
The airy zones, till thou art lost in highest!
 Upon the branch the laughing thrushes cling,
About her home the humble linnet wheels,
Around the tower the gathered starlings swing;
 These mix their songs and weave their figured reels :

Thou risest in thy lonely joy away,
From the first rapturous note that from thee steals,
  Quick, quick, and quicker, till the exalted lay
Is steadied in the golden breadths of light,
'Mid mildest clouds that bid thy pinions stay.
  The heavens that give would yet sustain thy flight,
And o'er the earth for ever cast thy voice,
If but to gain were still to keep the height.
  But soon thou sinkest on the fluttering poise
Of the same wings that soared : soon ceasest thou
The song that grew invisible with joys.
  Love bids thy fall begin; and thou art now
Dropped back to earth, and of the earth again,
Because that love hath made thy heart to bow.
  Thou hast thy mate, thy nest on lowly plain,
Thy timid heart by law ineffable
Is drawn from the high heavens where thou shouldst reign
  Earth summons thee by her most tender spell;
For thee there is a silence and a song :
Thy silence in the shadowy earth must dwell,
  Thy song in the bright heavens cannot be long.
—And best to thee those fates may I compare
Where weakness strives to answer bidding strong.
      Lord Gerbert thought in Mano to prepare
An instrument for service high and great,
And for that end to unfold the truth did spare.
  Joanna's secret would he not repeat
In Mano's ear: the which great pity proved,
And therewithal he practised some deceit,
  Hoping, ere Mano knew that he was loved,
That in them both unnourished love would die—
All which fell otherwise than it behoved.

Sir Mano being passed forth, the next was I,
The writer of these things that here are told,
Who unto Gerbert entered and stood nigh.
 Truly most noble was he to behold :
His face was large and mild, his forehead wide,
His long robe fastened close with studs of gold.
 His piercing eyes o'erran with mighty pride :
At prime he was : strong-limbed, of stature high :
Nor yet to his head had Time his hand applied.
 Such was his presence, who now wondrously
Is carried round the world with dark renown,
And fears all men by his strange history.
  With him was set the archbishop of the town,
Of whom I spake above : whose life of sin
On his high order brought reproaches down.
 And their discourse, whenas I entered in,
Was turned on Mano : whom I heard anon
The vile one to calumniate begin,
 And wax in choler, Mano being one
Whom Thurold loved, whom this man deemed his foe
For deeds that in the long past had been done.
 Then gan in Gerbert's eyes the flame to glow ;
And on the other a strange look he bent,
" Better this good knight mayst thou one day know,"
 Said he, " And elsewhere be thy malice spent."
The other answered, " Wherefore now, I pray,
From thee to me is such a saying sent ? "
 And Gerbert answered, " Only this I say,
That least of all it fitteth thee to rail :
Nor all I know tell I to thee this day :
 But what I may I will : mark thou the tale.
A knight named Mannus, of the Lombards, who

CANTO XVII.] A POETICAL HISTORY. 57

Against the Saracen oft rode in mail,
  One day, being weary with long travel, drew
Nigh to a gentle river, where was seen
A cottage small, and a low raft thereto.
  There close beside the bank of grassy green
Lived a brave miller, who his babes maintained
By plying in the barge those banks between:
  His course he took wherever might be gained
Grist for his wheel, or would return the same.
And by his cottage this bold knight upreined;
  The little children there were at their game:
To whom he called with cheery voice and kind,
Bidding them hold his warhorse mild and tame,
  Whilst in the cot he might refreshment find.
Yet of them was there none that undertook
The mighty beast in their weak hold to bind:
  Till one from out the timid crowd forth broke,
A little boy, and on the bridle laid
His dauntless hand, that with no terror shook;
  And drew the great horse forward, nought dismayed
When his full breathing in his face he felt,
And saw his trampling feet: the knight then said,
  Well pleased, to the miller, that 'twere but ill dealt
That child so noble should no better be
Than they who in that humble dwelling dwelt.
  'Sir,' said the miller, 'he comes not of me
Albeit he among my children fare:
For 'tis seven years since I my barge set free,
  'And, floating homeward, found this tender care
Laid underneath the sacks that hold the corn;
But never knew what hand had left him there.
  'Not very long the infant had been born,

And him I reared for pity and for ruth.'
Then said the knight, 'Upon that babe forlorn
  'As thou hadst pity, this I say in sooth,
Thy pity shall repent thee not; for I,
As best I can, will recompense thy truth.'
  Then offered he much gold the child to buy
Whereto the miller presently agreed,
And bade his wife equip him thence to hie;
  Who brought him forth anon, and bade God speed,
Making some tears to come : and lastly when
The boy was lifted on the mighty steed,
  'From evil women keep him,' said she then;
And as with gathered bridle forth they rode,
The miller said, 'Keep him from evil men.'
      —" Then with that worthy knight the child abode,
For fifteen years, bearing his foster name,
When the knight died : then forth he took his road
  To Count Thuroldus, to whose camp he came
With many, whom the Italian venture brought
From other parts, and love of martial fame.
  He is a knight of courage high and haught,
But mild and courteous, just and temperate :
Right worthy are the deeds that he has wrought."
      —" But yet his birth, his rank and race relate,"
The other coldly answered : and return
Received from Gerbert, " For that knowledge wait,
  Because the tale may nearly thee concern
When I shall tell it : but another thing
Concerning Mano thou this day shalt learn :
  That to Saint Benedict an offering
Him from a child the good knight Mannus gave,
Wrapping within the altar's covering

His little hand : to keep which contract grave
'Tis mine to draw him from the worldly throng
By fatherly persuasion, and to save."
    This said, his eyes on the archbishop long
He bent with firmness and austerity,
The while to me his words he did prolong :
    And this the sum—that I should instantly
For Mano seek, and bid him be of heart
From Gerbert, and not muse on fantasy :
    And that to Gerbert's ear I should impart
Whate'er he did, still urging his return
Across the Alps by friendship's winning art.
    —This lesson then from Gerbert did I learn :
And further, that with Mano I should go
To Italy, and still with him sojourn :
    Right glad was I that it was ordered so.

END OF BOOK I

BOOK II.

BOOK II.

I.—HOW FERGANT WENT TO BE WITH MANO: AND OF OTHER THINGS.

LOVE teacheth many things, and answereth
To many questions which the soul outspieth;
Because that God is love, and witnesseth
   To his own image, in the soul which lieth:
Therefore in knowledge he doth most abound
Whoever upon love's strong pinion flieth.
   And when that love with fair success is crowned,
Then is man's state made perfect upon earth:
But most unhappiness in love is found.
   Then fullest plenty feels the curse of dearth;
And, if not worse, yet this is bitterer
Than to have tasted of love's sweets is worth.
   In that great knight whether should I prefer
Dolour or sweetness to have borne the sway
When I from Gerbert came as comforter?
   His eye fell fiercely on me, when my way
I found into his lodging and began
On some pretence some timid words to say.
   Full wroth he seemed, but as a gentle man:
And I observed that though he chafed at heart,

And balked anger through his pulses ran,
Yet neither Blanche nor Giroie's name did part
His lips with bitterness: to noble mind
Fate's fullest quiver holds not envy's dart.
　But Gerbert's name he shunned, as if unkind
His part herein had been : and, truth to own,
This first began their friendship to unbind.
　And when lord Gerbert's comfort I made known,
This seemed to stir him, and he would not hear:
Then silent sat I, while he chafed alone ;
　Till the rage seemed to leave him ; and with cheer
Quite altered, he gan suddenly to say
That thence to Italy his course was clear.
　Then, when I answered that my journey lay
Wherever his, he took it in good part,
And we made pact to travel the next day.
　　　Now in good truth I have not to impart
The time when Gerbert that sad marriage made
Which cast on Mano such a scald of heart:
　Nor whether rightly deemed himself betrayed
The knight, as having shown his love before
To Gerbert, and from him expecting aid.
　But a stern coldness certainly did lower
Upon his eyelids, whenso'er the thought
Of Gerbert came upon him in that hour.
　　　But this do I suspect, that all was wrought
By cunning of that damsel false and fair
Whom first from Italy Sir Mano brought,
　The wild Diantha, haunting everywhere,
And hating Mano in her secret mind,
Who for her ends no enginry would spare.
　She then, when Blanche and Giroie she divined

In secret wedlock to desire to be,
With Gerbert that strong knot to tie combined.
Not that for them she toiled; her industry
Was by their means to compass her desire,
And of all laws of God and man be free.
For this bad daughter of a better sire
With a vile losel dweller of the wild
Was playing now, drawn on by evil fire;
To whom she fled, and thence was domiciled
Long time in savagery with evil men,
And many a month from honesty exiled.
Of that adventure shall be heard again,
For much came of it: note ye only here,
When Gerbert lay at Rouen, that 'twas then.
For in that time, as after did appear
To me much searching, on some embassy
She came from Féchamp, where the others were.
Attended well she came, but secretly,
And saw lord Gerbert: then from thence alone
Into the widespread woods escaped hard by.
       Now as to Mano, who to me was known
More closely from the time that Gerbert bade
That I should share his expedition,
Concerning Mano thus much shall be said,
That he my love so drew that never I
What faults in him I noted open laid:
And when lord Gerbert questioned privily,
Of me he got but little: least of all
Upon that noble knight would I be spy.
For good his purpose was though great his fall,
When fiery passion, reason's opposite,
Working through subtle fate, did him inthrall.

F

He was of all the most for action fit;
The same contemplative, and highly wrought :
Magnanimous he was, and fine of wit.
  The practices of others feared he nought;
Placable as to open enmity,
But, once deceived, never to be resought.
  Never would he, save but for treachery
His friend forsake, or make his faith unsure
For vice or folly, or calamity.
  While Gerbert of mere friendship had less cure ;
Who held that there might come occasions great,
When even a good man might that name abjure;
  And that who feared himself to separate
From his best fellow, if the time were nigh,
Was but infirm, nor fit for things of state.
So diversely they held of amity.

II.—HOW MANO SET FORTH FOR ITALY.

THE next day after Mano had resumed
  His former cheer to me so suddenly,
When the first beam the ready sky illumed,
  Our common voyage into Italy
We gan to hasten: and I found thereto
That Mano had done much in secrecy.
  For he was one who what he would pursue
Achieved with little noise ; others there are
Whose tools are in their mouths, their work to do.
      Some marvels happened great and singular
Upon that voyage, which is now to tell,
Nigh the feared advent of Christ's second star.
  But nothing shall be told that not befell

In very truth, as God my Saviour be,
Albeit the truth full many shall repel.
 For wondrous truth is taken diversely :
With credence by the nobler is she met,
And bears fair issue to expectancy :
 Base things on her the baser sort beget.—
But here, to make short tale, with sundry men
Out of the town our early feet we set.
 Those who on travel with us entered then
Were they who to the venture had agreed ;
And on the road we took up more again.
 As we from town to town began proceed,
They waited for us all the way along,
Until we had as many as were need :
 And were at last above five hundred strong,
Poor knights the most, with servants two or three :
Few arms were seen this company among,
 Though arms there were : nor any bravery,
But all was hidden under pilgrim gown,
Ere the last following received had we ;
 Then we began to skirt round every town,
The safer so to hold upon our way,
Like simple pilgrims, clothed in black or brown.
 But neither signs were wanting to display
Peril to us, and evils manifold ;
For when we passed where the dark valley lay
 Of that poor peasant whose sad tale was told,
One that among us was in company
Felt his knees smitten with a senseless cold,
 And in his hips such pain, that like to die
From horse he fell to ground, nor could be raised
Ere that a monk, who was a priest, rode nigh,

And signed the cross upon the man amazed :
Whereon he forthy rose and sat upright :
And for his strange deliverance God be praised.
 This was the working of that evil wight
Who haunted in the lonely country there,
And made it ill to pass by day or night.
   Likewise to Paris when we gotten were,
There was strange darkness cast o'er every street,
And all was stiller than a sepulchre.
 Unlit the houses were : none did we meet,
When Mano with the men most near to him
Rode by that church which is Saint Dennis' seat :
 And, passing by the church door great and dim,
One of the men by hand invisible
Was smitten, that he loudly gan blaspheme,
 And rolled in raging madness from his sell.
Whereat the door was opened from within,
And a strong light upon the dark did swell.
 And a great man and woman there were seen,
Who knelt before the altar : there was none
Beside them in the church all trim and clean,
 Where service was prepared, and the altar shone
With gold and silver : he who then knelt there
Slowly arose, and issued forth anon :
 And we beheld that he a crown did wear ;
Large-faced and sad was he, of royal cheer :
And to that cursing one, whom black despair
 Had overwhelmed with madness, he drew near
And took him by the hand, and from the ground
Raised, and some secret words dropped in his ear.
  When, lo, the oppressed grew straightway sane and
    sound.

Then to Sir Mano said the man royal,
"Me, whom thou seest recure the sinner's wound,
 "And sweep the garner demoniacal,
Know for that king whom late the unkind decree
Of excommunication made to fall.
 "Robert am I; on whose head Gregory
Hath fulminated for the marriage made
With her who now is put away from me."
. Then Mano, "Hast thou then, sire king, obeyed
That hard compulsion? this much pities me."—
"Yea," the other said, "to Rome be this conveyed,
 "If thitherward, rider, thy journey be:
For all men fly from me and yon poor queen,
And on us both the curse sits heavily:
 "To us and to our land it happens e'en
As if the leprosy upon us lay.
This tell in Rome which thou hast heard and seen,
 "King Robert and his wife now put away:
Her, to whose former son at baptism I
By sponsorship contracted in new way
 "A fatal kinship, full of mystery;
Becoming by that rite to him, 'twas said,
More than a father in affinity;
 "And to his mother, whom my wife I made,
Akin within prohibited degree:
Which sin of ignorance is against me laid.
 "Say that thou hast beheld my penalty,
Say that thou hast beheld us lying here
In penitential woe and misery.
 "For with the morning's light we shall appear
No more as man and wife in all men's sight;
But first before the people taste that cheer

"To which the Saviour doth his own invite,
Then part for evermore : this final woe
Remains to us with coming of the light."
   Then Mano answered, "If it must be so,
Nor better may be, I shall do thy mind,
Since I to Rome am mainly bent to go;
   "But wroth am I, oh king, pious and kind,
That German pope, imperial minion,
On thee should have this power to loose and bind."
   Then back into the church the king anon
His heavy steps betook; and from the gate
Sir Mano rode, and on his way was gone.
         Thence onward we traversed the kingdom great
Of Burgundy; which Eudes, queen Bertha's son,
That son who caused king Robert's wretched fate,
   Thought lately from the empire to have won,
But lost his life in battle : and, I ween,
With him that kingdom ever is foredone.
   There in our passage through the land were seen
On every knoll and rock the castles high
Of the great seigneurs each in his domain:
   There wretched serfs at labour in the eye
Of the hard villicus on every plain,
We saw in the shadow of each sovereignty.
   We saw at every dawn the struggling train
From their small hamlets led to drudge the day,
And by the ganger urged with heavy pain.
   They who thus toiled in pitiful array,
By night were hutted into noisome fold,
And, being forbidden lights, in darkness lay.
   Their only light, the sun, did they behold,
Their great taskmaster rising in the east,

From course diurnal into annual rolled ;
Their days into their lives with toil increased.
Ah, Lord, how many days saw we that throng
In garments drab, with cramped limbs uneased !
We saw their faces dark with hopeless wrong ;
And oftentimes their lords with merry cheer
Drove their brave hunts the wretched troop among:
    And on our way there fell this omen drear.
Riding by night (as it was our usage,
Whenever to a city we drew near)
    That we might safer make our pilgrimage,
We skirted round a city great and high ;
But with the morning held a plain voyage :
    Where in the open land beneath the sky,
Walking around a lake's inclosing bank,
Behold of half-clad men a company !
    Long spears they bore, which into the deep tank
They still pushed down among the sedge and reeds.
Then Mano said to me : "Mark yon poor rank,
    And know thou whence that industry proceeds.
They walk the fishpond with their staves all night,
Seeking the places where the frog most breeds,
    Whose chanting might their masters' sleep affright."—
While thus he spake, there came a mournful cry
From those half-clothed purveyors of delight ;
    And when we turned the occasion to descry,
Behold in that strange fishing one had struck
His spear into a bundle, which on high
    The reeds held from the wave : the cruel hook
Was bedded in an infant's tender breast,
Exposed through want : such prey such angle took.
    This to the pale-faced fisher drew the rest :

And in the gasping babe that fisher found
One whom his own life did with life invest.
  Fast then a priest of ours came to the ground,
The sacrament of baptism to apply:
But, ere he reached, in death the babe was wound.
  No sign more evil could have been, perdy;
But in this very thing, of which I tell,
Many concerning Mano strangely lie:
  That in his arms was found a child of hell,
A demon under form of infant dead,
Which, ere the holy drops upon it fell,
  Shrank suddenly to nought, and vanished:
Of all which not a jot by me was seen,
Who present was, and all things witnessed,
And should have known, if such a thing had been.

III.—WHAT BEFELL IN THE ALPS.

NOW entered we among that desert pile
  That overhangs with steeps the Italian plain:
By many a craggy way and long defile
  Ascending through the passes of the chain.
Hard was that voyage: colder grew the air;
On either hand the dark trees seemed in pain,
  And strove their stiffened branches to upbear:
At every turn came forth the mountain mass,
Girded with pines, snow-wrapped, with brows severe:
  But higher when we clomb the endless pass,
Then the locked mountains either hand that stood
Met knee to knee; and passage scarce there was.
  Then, lest the hillmen who thereby abode
Should stay the march of larger company,

Sir Mano bade us some to quit the road,
And them who kept it to go two and three;
The more, because the savage Saracens
Held stations on the side next Italy.
Wherefore along that Alpine region thence
We rode divided : Mano for his part
Turned sharply toward the nighest eminence;
And him I followed from the road apart,
Ascending steeply, with some few beside,
And slowly travelling the mountain swart.
Thus mounting to the top we gan to ride
O'er stony places clogged with frozen snow,
A dreadful desert, through the which no guide
Of kindly voice heartened our footsteps slow :
In clouds the pale sun hung, which more and more
Gathered, and caused a dusk o'er all to grow;
And the white waste changed colour : then down bore
Of thick and heavy snow a hideous fall,
Through which we went in blindness evermore.
Then each to other full of fear did call,
For every step was frightful in that waste,
Where prospect was obliterated all,
Nor now indeed knew we to halt or haste;
And painfully our trembling beasts we drew,
Which were by demons into terror cast,
Who with strange sounds and voices round us flew,
And opened chasms suddenly at our feet,
And stones against us from each quarter threw.
But God of all their malice made defeat,
For when for hours we had suffered this distress,
The darkness, and the storm that on us beat,
At last the fiends had spent their wickedness,

And the blithe sun looked out on our array,
What time he sought the Hesperian recess :
 He cast on us a golden beam full gay,
But darkened into blood-red, as he sank,
And left the heavens purple and curdled grey :
 Then we refitted our equipments dank.
But, soon was turned to woe our brief delight.
Mano himself was missing from our rank,
 Nor anywhere beheld we him in sight,
Nor search nor shout recovered him to us :
Upon our bootless toils came down the night,
And wrapped us on the summit ruinous.

IV.—OF AN ADVENTURE WHICH FELL TO MANO.

ANOTHER day and night was passed before
 We found that leader, in whose valiant eyes
Lay all the safety that we might explore :
 Then, as we journeyed sadly at sunrise,
We came upon him riding loftily,
Clad in his knightly arms without disguise,
 No seeming pilgrim now : by him, perdy,
A gallant lady in rich raiment dight
With hand right skilful and with looks full free
 Was managing her courser proud and light.
Together came they pricking o'er the hill,
And great amazement filled us at the sight.
 But in my heart arose the fear of ill :
For altered seemed the knight in look and mind,
When that he joined us, who for him stood still.
 And how he chanced that lady brave to find
In that wild desert, must by me be told,

Whom in the tempest he had left behind.
 He by adventure in the darksome cold
Passed onward o'er the summits wild and vast,
As he beyond us was both strong and bold :
 And when the evil tempest first was past,
He found himself upon the shoulder broad
Of a great mountain, that was skyward cast.
 Where straight before him, to the sky a load,
On a great horse, a knight with mighty spear,
Stood on the last verge which the mountain showed,
 Who called to him, that he should come anear.
" For," said that knight, " heaven sends thee to my aid ;
Quick, quick ! behold a double danger here,—
 " One who to meet me single is afraid,
As best I guess, albeit to fight alone
On this lone shore our covenant was made."
 Even while he spake, two men at hand were shown
Riding right swiftly from the ground beneath :
And Mano fixed himself against the one
 Who next him with his long spear threatened death.—
The spear hits full upon his armed breast,
Yet with weak force ; and on the ground lieth :
 But Mano's stroke, which lighted on the crest,
Bore down the other, though without a wound,
From horse ; and he, stretched out, the cold earth pressed.
 Whereat right quickly leaping to the ground,
Sir Mano loosed his helm : and, lo, a rain
Of long bright hair fell loosened all around :
 As when from sheaf of yellow ripened grain
The thresher tears the bond wherewith 'twas bound,
That beauty broke to light upon the plain.
 And lo, within the vizor's iron round

A pale and swooning face, and in the mail
A woman's tender form and limbs were found :
Who, as her senses had begun to fail.
Now sank the more, the less she was embraced
In the iron prison, and waxed still more pale.
  Then Mano feared the strength that he had cast
Into his blow : and was about to lend
What aid he might in pity and in haste :
When he beheld him whom he did befriend
Thrown to the ground by his strong enemy,
Who was in act to make of him an end.
 Which when he saw, thither full fast ran he,
And with strong blows compelled the foe to turn,
Who faced him thereupon right stubbornly.
 And long they fought, till Mano, who did burn
To achieve that part, with heaped strokes him slew,
And to the others minded to return.
 Ah, then a piteous sight came to his view,
When back he went to seek that woman fair ;
Behold, the knight for whom his sword he drew,—
He saw him hold the woman by her hair,
Crushing her with his foot, and thrusting deep
His sword into her throat, helplessly bare.
 He could not stay it, the precious blood did leap,
The race was won by death ere he came nigh :
" Murderer, as thou hast sown thou now shalt reap."
 He spake in rage, and moved with menace high,
When, lo, the other cast his sword away,
And smilingly his onset dared defy :
 And saying, " Such light crime I well can pay,"
Therewith cast off her helmet : and down fell
Long locks, as fair as those on ground that lay.

Then piece by piece her arms did she compel
To drop from her, and at the last stood free
A glorious lady, whose round form did swell
   So fair and full, that marvel seemed to be
That man's straight armour her round limbs had cased.
In a white, close-made garment clad was she,
   Which held her delicately from feet to waist;
And in all beauty there for eye to see
Some time she stood displayed: then with slow haste
   She turned, and with the show of modesty,
Back to her horse withdrew for shrouding gown,
While stood that knight disordered verily.
   He was by passion driven up and down
Between the dead and living, both so fair.
Him sometimes horror and amazement drown,
   Then other thoughts: then death's dread presence there,
The bleeding corpse and trodden ground, down bore
All else that rose his heaving breast to share.
   And all this ill within him wrought so sore,
As when a tall tree in the stormy wind
This way and that is lashed with angry roar.
   From this to that he looked with troubled mind:
But last with hoarse demand to her he cries,
Asking what cause such cruel deed could find.
   She then, with robe still loose, her stedfast eyes,
Filled with a seeming fear, toward him hied,
And thus began her tale.
            " The injuries,
   If they be cause enough thou shalt decide,
Whose valiant hand hath helped me in my need,
The injuries I bore. I was a bride :

My lover known by many a noble deed :
(His bride I was, alas, but am no more,)
By name Ramengo, who this region freed
    From the Arab robber, the idolater,
Who in his yearly fleets the sea o'errides,
And to the hills ascending from the shore,
    In fixed camps on this poor land abides :
Of whom a numerous band, by demons sped,
Caught my brave love within the hill's deep sides,
    When all alone, by fatal valour led,
Within their bounds he rode on enterprise :
Him there they overwhelmed, and left him dead.
    " To me my brother came with tears and sighs,
And told me how he found him lying there
Slain, but not stripped : and bade me to arise,
    That I with him the corpse away might bear.
I learned of him the place : from him I took
His arrows keen, nor further let him fare :
    Alone on me that quest I undertook,
Mounted my swift horse, rode, and laboured through
The changed hills unto the bloody nook :
    There found I dead him whom alive I knew :
Nor long in ambush waited, ere drew near
A wretch, who off my dead love's armour drew.
    That stealthy wretch but made himself appear
Truer my arrow's mark : the husband he
Of her, the woman who now lieth here.
    Into his breast my bolt went verily :
And I put on those arms which he to bear
From the dead body had begun to wry.
    Likewise the caitiff's armour did I tear
From his false back, and on his own horse pile ;

And so rode through the hostile valley near.
His hut I found fixed midst his people vile,
Clad was I in his mantle striped and red,
To avoid his cursed people by that wile.
Thus to his door I rode, and loudly said
Unto the woman who there sat within,
' My husband by thy husband's side lies dead,
Both lying in the hills with naked skin.
Spoils bring I, but not such thou dost divine,
Nor am I that I seem these trappings in.
' My husband his hand slew who fell by mine.
Take here this bloody mantle : take to thee
Thy husband's arms and horse : take that is thine :
' And armed therewith come thou and fight with me,
Who will await thee on the high mountain
Alone, till death shall cease our enmity.'
Woman to woman never doth complain :
And she without a cry from me received
The challenge and the robe in dumb disdain ;
Nor showed herself how suddenly bereaved :
But, as I rode away, in my mind's eye
Her dreadful look of hate I apperceived :
And suddenly, and with perplexity
Upon some treachery my thought was cast,
Which might on me be practised secretly.
And now for combat in the desert vast
Alone I stood upon the high mountain :
Far, far beneath whose height those clouds were massed,
Which on the vale were spending their thick rain :
The while like herds the rocks in vaporous wreath
Rested apart : and nought my eyes at strain
Could see, nor pierce the misty sea beneath.

Long waited I, and then dread horror shook
My body, and the mighty fear of death:
  So that almost my hand the spear forsook,
And my horse fretted: still while terror bore
Down to the hostile valley my keen look,
  The rising wind the vaporous curtain tore:
And two black forms I saw bounding with speed
To mount the opposing hill from that low shore.
  Full fast they came; and now I knew indeed
The treacherous odds that in my heart I feared;
Wildly I turned to flee: when, at my need,
  The noble knight, my rescuer, appeared.
Why tell I more, brave lord? thy hand of might
(For whose stout rescue be the heavens revered)
  Her brother's soul hath sent to endless night:
Her brother, summoned by that traitress dead
Against a woman in unequal fight.
  Judge therefore thou, whether unmerited
The vengeance which against her I did use.
  And if thou answer, Yea: my blood to shed
By thy thrice worthy hand I nought refuse."

V.—HOW WE CAME INTO ITALY.

BETWIXT or vice or virtue ye who live
  The trembling balanced life, both pure and frail,
Will ye not to that man some pity give
  Whomever dark temptations do assail?
Or doth the leaf still hanging on the bough
Laugh at his brother driven down the gale?
  Another blast, and it alike may bow.
From you I ask for pity, and not scorn:

Shame's touch in turn may redden every brow.
  Brave Mano now, full long of love forlorn,
Turned greedily to solace wild and free,
Seeming to have the thought of Blanche outworn.
  Love's rebel he against love's tyranny;
For hope being gone left the soul desolate,
And the heart ready for conspiracy.
  Now came occasion : now was sent by fate
This woman terrible, whose haughty will
And shameless daring matched her beauty great.
  Her cruel story, all contrary still
To what he knew of women, on him threw
A deadly charm and irresistible ;
  And to the same effect and purpose drew
His own part in that story : he gan fail
From his youth's purity ; and evil knew :
  And miserable desires pierced his mind's mail,
Though love erewhile so fitted close his heart,
That nought of base to enter might avail :
  Love from that fort had governed every part.
But now that false-named love, that regent vile,
Whose drunken shaft usurps the fire-winged dart,
  With lust for reverence, and for honour guile,
Worked in him reckless mood, and unrestraint,
And changed his mien from what it was erewhile.
  Now in our journeying the hills more faint
Lay far and white behind us, and the way
Turned downward to the plain by passes quaint.
  Known were those paths from earth's primæval day
To such rude men which in those hills abode :
But we passed fairly without check or stay.
  Pace with the streams we kept, that marked the road,

G

And thus descending looked on valleys fair
Enlaced with terraced vines, that darkly glowed.
The purple sky, high rolled in æstive air,
The grass, the budded flowers gave more delight,
The laughing bursten broom seemed yellower.

And now our scattered fellows gan unite,
Where the long passes ended; and the way
Suddenly brought the Italian plain in sight,

The glorious golden country, for whose sway
Fierce nations strive : yea, even as the shores
Lead to the boundless sea, and therewith stay;

So suddenly the hills their rocky doors
Behind us shut, and left us on that plain,
Which, like the sea, rolled far his swelling floors.

There vine and olive-crested grass and grain :
Cities, the Roman works, stood fair and high,
Like islands, in the golden-billowed main.

This glorious sight brought joy to every eye :
But in our hearts was woe and trouble found
Because of Mano and that harlotry.

He in that woman's snare a slave was bound :
All day by her he rode in disarray,
And their loud laughter did the vales confound.

For nought beside vain dalliance cared they,
And their light folly was before our eyes,
Which mixed in our contentment sore dismay.

Those of our pilgrims who were good and wise,
The holy men who on this quest repaired,
Were often mocked by her with gaieties.

For in the toilsome march they never spared
Of prayers, fastings, and austerity,
And, as they rode, to stripes their shoulders bared,

Or read in holy books, which verily
Good store they carried on each patient beast,
To solace them with godly history:
   All which full oft she turned to scurril jest.
Thus murmurs grew among us day by day,
Though fear of Mano still their voice repressed.
   But one thing only of her evil play
Shall here be told: that she to Mano gave
A talisman, that in her bosom lay;
   A broidery of colours bright and brave,
But stained with a blot of sanguine hue:
Which she had plucked out of the sudden grave,
   Where that fair body lay the which she slew.
She gave it him but as a gift of price,
Nor told him from what wealth her gift she drew.
   Fair was the cloth, and wrought in costly wise:
And from the same in time great marvel fell,
Ere we had quittance of her sorceries.
   Thus travelled we the plain, e'en as I tell:
Nor long behind us Gerbert left the land
Whence we so far were come: he steering well
   By sea to avoid the Saracenic band,
Which we atween the hills had safely passed,
Arrived before us on the Roman strand:
And there it was we met him at the last.

VI.—OF A BATTLE WITH THE SARACENS: AND OF OUR COMING TO A LOMBARDIAN TOWN.

NOW when our road left that high mountain stage,
    And issued fair on the Lombardian plain,
The Saracens came on us, full of rage
    That we had passed unspied their guardian chain.
And this last storm fell furious on our rear.
But soon our horsemen charged back amain,
    And through the valley long, at point of spear
Repelled them : and so hotly them pursued,
That to their hills they wished themselves more near.
    Thus in this region was again made good
The Norman fighting, which doth still prevail
O'er all that hath in war against it stood,—
    The Saracen's curved sword and light-wrought mail,
The Teuton's straight sword and thick-forged plates,
The Greekish spear and targe : for, scale on scale
    Of iron upon canvas stitched in plaits,
Strong and yet agile, swift but close in fight,
So clad 'gainst all himself the Norman mates.
    We held the field and all confessed our might :
And, victory with little pain achieved,
We moved toward a town which rose in sight.
    And to that pleasant place we were received
Right willingly by the Lombardian men,
Who through great fear had their high walls upheaved,
    And from tall castles overlooked the plain :
Dreading an enemy more fierce and fell
Than the Alpine foe, than e'en the Saracen.
    For here the Ungrian, who doth all excel
In cruelty and greed, still makes his road,

And drives the Lombard to his citadel.
  Scarce might the land be tilled ; and no abode
Outside the walled city lay secure :
The farmer in the walls his crop bestowed,
  Then guarded it in arms : glad to immure
In the ripe season what his pains had sown :
For oftener the sowings immature
  His hand was forced to reap ere they were grown.—
Ah, grass and leaves may flourish all the year,
But corn and fruit one season only own.
    So entered we, as bringing hope to fear,
And strength to weakness : and with welcome kind
Our leader was received, and gentle cheer.
  And some days there did we refreshment find ;
And walked the streets amid the people there,
The Huns being gone with the cold wintry wind.
  For frost was ceased from out the pleasant air :
The blue sky shone with those white clouds of Spring
Which the mild shepherd Zephyr drives with care ;
  That herd whose sweet milk fattens everything.
Such pleasantness we found within the walls
Which now begirt us with their lofty ring :
  And the new-leaved trees hard by the halls
Where we were lodged, rose sweetly in the sky ;
And in them made full many a bird his calls,
  And from love's unseen echo got reply.—
So pleasant was the place which was the seat
Of the great teacher of an heresy ;
  For here abode that sophist false but sweet,
Vilgardus named, surnamed Grammarian,
Whose errors in all lands did Fame repeat.
  Even he it was, of whom the story ran

That in the guise of poets to him came
The fiends by night, and seized upon the man:
  Who thenceforth wicked blasphemies gan frame,
And everywhere the same with zeal to spread:
Whereby full many fell to sword and flame.
    Him in this town we found, it is no dread:
An aged man, yet fresh as any child,
Bearing white hairs upon his ruddy head;
  Firm-eyed, and of behaviour sweet and mild;
So that of him but little would be thought
That many his false teaching had beguiled.
  And in those days Sir Mano to him sought,
And held with him much converse; which in part
I heard; and of the rest by Mano taught,
The sum of all I shall to you impart.

VII. — CONCERNING VILGARDUS, SURNAMED
GRAMMATICUS.

THIS aged man, this old heresiarch,
  Would in his pleasant parlour often sit,
Until the setting light made gentler dark;
  And with Sir Mano talk with pleasant wit:
Or with me also, if it happened so;
For he to conference would all admit.
  And he would bid his Rhetian wine to flow,
Which he, from Virgil, boasted not to vie
With the Falernian, more than he outgo
  That divine master in philosophy.
For of the ancients still he made his song,
Whose books to hold in fear and enmity,

Their store of fables full of lust and wrong,
I have been still instructed by my rule,
Nor ever were they suffered us among:
Though Gerbert, it is certain, and the school
Of men less strict, in favour held the same,
Till some said that in love their hearts were cool.
　But that old sophister put off all shame,
Teaching what seemed against our holy faith,
To turn the world back from the Christian name.
　" Behold," said he, " this age so full of death!
This age is full of woe; this age is sick,
Discoloured, as a fish that gasps for breath
　" Beside the waters, where it darted quick.
It cannot breathe the air of heaven fine ;
But cast it back into the water thick,
　" And it revives 'mid the delicious brine.—
So ye, who live this age of woe and fear,
Too high are lifted on the shore divine.
　" Ye wait the coming of the thousandth year,
And fly from nature's sea to gasp of heaven,
Believing that the end of all is near.
　" Would ye breathe heaven, and be with angels even,
Being yet men ?　Or think ye that your eyes
Can leave that strife to which ye all are given,
　" And see the true heaven-colours in yon skies,
Unmixed with bloody fire, black specks and motes,
And what else in true sight are maladies ?
　" Not so : the shoal that in the ocean floats
Sees better the fair sky through waters grey,
With lazy eyes set in their shagreen coats.
　" Plunge down again : back to your deep, away !
Find life within the succourable wave,

Nor struggle thence, where nature bids you stay.
"So in the glimmering vastness shall ye have
Heaven's pictures, or of cloud or vacancy,
Moving above you in their pageant brave.
"Ye, who can think for all, hearken to me.
This age is writ in woe, in horror sealed,
Because true bounds no more observed be,—
"Those chancels of the universal field
Of thought and action, which the old sages raised
And left, of man for ever to be held.
"A thousand years the Grecian sages gazed
On happiness, on virtue, on the best,
On all those actions for which men are praised.
"Then one arose, the master of the rest,
Grave Aristotle, whom ye too revere,
And to all questions laid his searching test.
"He meted limits with his line severe;
By reason studying both the soul and things:
And sweet the fields he fenced with knowledge clear:
"The soul may enter there, and fold her wings
In peace. What know ye more, that ye should dare
Mix his firm thoughts with vain imaginings?
"Uproot the landmarks, which he planted there,
With theologic reasons, and insert
Cognitions, sanctions of religion, where
"Only those seeds of Truth grow without hurt
Which man in his own being still may find,
And which by being known to good convert,
"And need no other force? Why make all blind
By mixing these with what religion gives
As to a being not to earth confined?"
    But what he said of Him who ever lives,—

That God being known the highest entity,
Whom science for her utmost term receives,
  No further than that word needs man to pry,
Since more than that to science cannot be ;—
Frustrating therefore all theology ;—
  Of this no more shall be set forth by me,
But that the man forgot in arguing so
That man's best study out of reach set he,
  And all the other sciences laid low :—
If the infinite perfection severed be
From man's pursuit, nought profits man to know.
  No more, I say, shall be set forth by me :
But rather toward the human arts I turn,
Where I of his discourse may be more free.—
  "Poetry sighs from out her buried urn,
With her fair sisters, who were once alive.—
Dig in this soil ; the streets ye tread upturn,
  "A thousand things from burial ye shall rive,—
Long broken marbles large and mild and sweet ;
Old walls, whereon the colours yet survive :
  "A world of death is trodden by your feet.
Seek in the homes of books—fear not to seek—
And wondrous are the things that ye shall meet :
  "The Roman Muses telling of the Greek
With native voice, in measures fair and full,
Ere that the last return themselves to speak.
  "Then shall ye know in ways how wonderful
The tracts of all the arts of old were laid,
Which change can alter not, nor time annul.
  "They are the best : they, like the hills, were made
At once with mighty sweep, ever to last,
By those who first to shape their forms essayed.

"Walk therefore in the footsteps of the past,
As they once walked, who only added more
To fill the spaces of those outlines vast

"Left by their fathers, who did first explore :
Ere on the world came that great change of mind,
Altering the face of things that was before,

" Dipping the world in ruin, making blind
The eyes that saw so clear, in miseries
Drowning the long-stored gatherings of mankind.

" This eateth up all health with strange disease :
And now, behold, this iron age doth wait
To see the end ! Truly the end it sees :

" For all is gone that blesses mortal state ;
This age of dark religion, in whose frown
Man sees on earth the heaven he fears to hate :

" Man, shuddering at the clouds that thicken down,
Might yet be happy, wretched though he be,
And bid those floods, his seedling hopes that drown,

" Roll back into the illimitable sea,
Nor have with their dark storm his sky bewept,
If but religion kept her own degree.

—" Her own degree if but religion kept,
Usurping not the arts and sciences,
Which she by aidance false hath overstepped.

"She hath her own domain, and great she is,
Which to diminish, that be far from me :
Nay, rather I establish her, I wis,

"More than the others who cry heresy ;
And what she is, perchance, know more than they.
Yea, rather would I name her Piety,

" And to be most divine of all would say,
And teach the things to her which appertain :

Nor was she known, how great, before Christ's day.
"Then heaven to earth descending made her
   plain :
And truth it is that not by any sage
That wrote of duty, neither by the strain
"Of poet carried through the Muse's rage,
Was pity shown to misery and pain.
Their work was not to alleviate nor assuage.
   "And Moral Virtue, neither may she deign
To mortal griefs, being raised on rectitude,
To point how man may happiness obtain.
   "Well she instructs the already wise and good :
But if this man or that incurably
Fail of her mark, being ignorant and lewd,
   "Or otherwise in mind or bodily
Unfit for duties, pity shows she none,
Nor bears the load of imbecility :
   "But out of hope she setteth such an one.
So be it : she herself is justified
By her own laws in her conclusion.
   "Let her alone ; be it her part to guide
To her own mark the capable and strong :
Nor let Religion touch her proper pride.
   "The arts, and all Apollo's learned throng
Teach life to man ; and their own use they have :
But they accept unhappiness and wrong
   "The half of their domain : without the grave
And mournful part of life what were they all ?
'Tis theirs to paint, not punish : show, not save.
   "And Contemplation, which doth man recal
To high beginnings, and is man's last force
To apprehend the things celestial,

" Must her own ladder bring, nor have recourse
To aught of outward or supernal aid :
For what is in the stream was in the source.
" What man his own by his own thought hath made
That only in his science he may know;
And by that instrument new realms invade.
" Man's own wings bear him whither he would go :
His arts, his thought, to strict conclusions bent,
Only take heed of weakness, pain, and woe,
" As what is either to them aliment,
Or else what hostile in the world is found,
Their perfect operation to prevent.
" But, lo, Religion from beyond the bound
Of art and thought enters our mortal state,
Piteous of man, and takes her special ground.
" What man in man sees but with awe or hate
She makes her own by right; the wretch she sees
Not to destroy, but to compassionate :
" Not for the spectacle of tragedies,
But for the hand of help : weakness and pain
Her province are ; her art to succour these.
" If ye knew this, such godliness were gain :
Nor would ye mix her with the functions right
Of the arts and sciences, to make all vain ;
" Nor would it be too simple and too trite
To call her mercy and humanity,
Since she was only seen by heaven's own light;
" Neither by science was it given to see,
Nor by man's art, how main this principle,
How lofty piteousness and charity.
" The arts and sciences their fields kept well,
Defenced with the walls that round them rose,

Of old time, high and indestructible.
" But, as a door new opened in a close,
Showing a garden fair beyond the wall
Which customarily the scene doth close,
" Delights the gazer, till more usual
The view becomes ; and, mingled with the rest,
Alone no longer doth the eye enthral :
" Even so Religion seen at first was best,
And from all else was counted separate,
And her especial function manifest :
" But long confounded since her primal date,
Zealots and bigots with contentious rage
Into her speech their ignorance translate :
" These blot with tears and blood her lovely page ;
So that her name is sorrow now and fear :
Nor doth she now man's highest thoughts engage :
" For they must worship less, who would revere."
  Thus mixing half truths in faith's mysteries
(As others since) spake that old sophister :
  And whoso hearkened to his subtleties ,
Found them most sweet ; and, in delusion wound,
The vulgar framed of them worse blasphemies.
  He let the water out, which ran around.
For in all lands, whither his words had course,
Perverters vile did presently abound :
  Robbers, who seized church goods without remorse :
New lights, who still were crying charity,
And took the poor men's dues by fraud or force :
  Wretches, who called religion piety,
And into every vilest trespass ran :
These through his words their crimes did multiply.
Such only good Vilgardus did to man.

VIII.—HOW THE UNGRIANS BESIEGING THE TOWN WERE BEATEN OFF.

AS in the mountain region even storms
      Seem part of a great peacefulness that spreads
From hill to hill o'er all the heavy forms
   Of rocks, that lift to heaven their rugged heads:
   So in that old man's speech, while we could hear
The dropping honey which persuasion sheds,
      And his enthusiastic eyes were near,
With their strange glances fixed on each in turn,
Less visible his errors did appear.
   But though the poisoned shafts did inly burn,
Yet some there were who to the truth were true,
Among our holy band, who whispered stern.
   Then cold looks passed, which soon to danger grew:
Whereat Sir Mano rising on his feet,
His heavy sword upon the table threw,
      Bidding all leave their threatenings to repeat
Against that aged man whose guests they were:
Whereon the murmurs rose to clamour great,
   And soon a quarrel raged, as ye shall hear,
Which afterwards came near calamity,
And wrought us at the time to troublous fear.
   A knight, who late had joined in Italy,
Waxed loud against both Mano and Vilgard:
And at the last their fury ran so high,
   That he with all his following prepared
To leave our quest, and rather join the foe,
Or stay behind, the city's walls to guard.
   Which Mano scorning, bade him stay or go:

And forthwith went he out, nor more was seen ;
But soon 'twas heard (a loss of little woe)
That he had stolen away the gallant quean,
With whom Sir Mano dallied in that day :
And with his following was escaped clean.
 When the next morning spread on earth her ray,
The plain stood thick with the wild Ungrian clan ;
Who with the night came up their siege to lay :
 They round the city, when the day began,
Uplifted to the sky their horrid shout,
And shot their cruel arrows as one man.
 Above the walls they searched the woodwork stout
Which the townsmen atop with beams made shift to shore :
Then with all speed their horses wheeled about,
 And from the walls their riders safely bore,
Preventing aim : wherefore in little space
The town in this game made the losing score.
 Then through the streets the priests and monks gan pace
In their procession, chanting litanies,
And mounting to the walls took there their place.
 " Ab Ungerorum nos tu jaculis
Defendas, Domine," loudly did they cry ;
" Et libera nos ab his miseriis."
 These ethnicks are the world's calamity :
In turms they shoot their arrows with strange speed,
And still upon their nimbleness rely :
 All other nations they in this exceed.
And, in their sieges, first the walls they clear,
With darts, then in a trice fresh troops succeed,
 Who to the vacant height their ladders rear,
And climb before the rally ; in meanwhile
Against surprise fresh horsemen close the rear.

And with their open arms was joined this guile,
That with their camp they carried conjuror Jews,
Who used by night this incantation vile :
    For they believe those spots, which whoso views
The changeful moon may mark in her pale sphere,
The old Shechinah which their race did lose :
    And from what look they wear, cloudy or clear,
They read the future, and by dull or bright,
And by the stars that nearest them appear.
    The devil gives them knowledge of this sleight;
And they instruct the heathen the best hours
Against the Christians to prevail in fight.
    And these had taken now this city's towers
Save but for fortune, which by God's decree
Within the sweep of Fate's all-dragging powers
    Reserves in earth's events contingency,
And this or that, with heart prudential
Against the set of things drives diversely :
    As now was seen, in that it did befall
That in those threatened towers the Normans lay;
Who, when the ladders hung upon the wall,
    Disdaining to be brought like beasts to bay,
Neither took part nor heed of danger near,
But issued from the gates in thick array.
    Upon the foe they set in hot career,
And drove away in clouds the Ungrian horse,
For all went down before the Norman spear.
    They hold the field : and, traversing in course,
The gathering squadrons break with slaughter great.
Then those upon the wall, put in fresh force,
    The ladders and the climbers overset
With mighty noise : when, as their wont it is

Suddenly to prevail or else retreat,
The Ungrians broke, and left their enterprise.
Thus stood the victory in all parts sure,
And far the Normans drove their enemies;
But when their burdened horses might endure
No more, they with small loss repassed the gate.
And so by them the town was made secure
Against the nigh approach of evil fate.

IX.—CONCERNING A KNIGHT WHOM MANO MET IN THE BATTLE.

UPON the field, when Mano put to flight
   The Ungrian enemy, as hath been told,
He found himself encountered by a knight
   Of Italy, who met with him full bold :
And yet when but few strokes were struck, and both
Full breathed as yet, on sudden cried he, " Hold !
" Say first what favour of the embroidered cloth
Unto the camail hangs from thy high crest."—
" None," answered Mano, " that should make thee loth
" In battle with me for to do thy best :
From her it is who once deluded me,
And whom too well thou knowest : guard now thy breast."
(He wore the token of that lady free,
Till him he found with whom she fled away :
And well he knew that knight of Italy.)
   Then heaved his sword : yet cried the other, " Stay !
There is no other napkin upon earth
Like that which in thy helm I see to-day.
   " My foster-sister wore it, whom from birth

I and my brothers knew on yonder hill.
Blood-stained I see it : if thou be of worth,
 "Say whence it bears those bloody signs of ill."
Then Mano, " Now to me doth truth appear :
Thy leman did thy foster-sister kill."
 The other then, " This strife a while forbear,
That elsewhere I may that dear blood requite."
Then Mano, " Rather stand thou fast for her
 " Whom, like a thief, thou took'st away by night."
The other said, " I will go far as thou
In any noble deed and proof of might :
 " Grant therefore to me what I ask thee now,
The meaning of thy doubtful words declare,
Which cause my hand to pause, my heart to bow."
 Then Mano told of her who arms did wear
On the hill; for whom he cast another down,
Who likewise seemed a knight in armour fair,
 Whom yet he spared : but who, when he was gone
To meet another champion, cruelly
Was put to death by the first-named one ;
 Who stabbed her in the neck without mercy,
And took that curious napkin from her throat,
As now he guessed, but knew not formerly.
 Then said the knight, " In turn I bid thee note
The history that I to thee shall show,
What to my father chanced in days remote.
 As he one day into the woods did go,
Where the pine-forests on yon mountains spread,
He heard a woman's voice in wailing low :
 Long hearkened he, while weary, and nigh dead
It sounded : but he stood in doubtful fear
By some hill-woman to be murdered :

The which hath happed ere now in places drear
To wandering knight, by shrieks and piteous moans
Drawn into woody brake and tangled brere,
  And there rent piecemeal, when the mournful tones
Were changed to yells, and his torn body there
Reeled into bleeding flesh and white-seen bones.—
  Of this he thought, but soon took better cheer;
And, following, found indeed a woman laid,
Whose groans were carried by the heedless air.
  Upon her empty breast an infant played:
And, questioned, she complained, 'Of Normandy
Am I: but of that land shall nought be said:
  'For that land was my peace and innocency.
Oh! let my dying heart a while yet hold,
Then break in this hard land of Italy.
  'Nay, of both lands my story must be told:
For from the one, expelled by traitorous love,
Hither I came with sorrows manifold;
  'Here nature by my torment doubly throve;
For at one birth two babes of me were born,
A boy, and this soon to be nestless dove.
  'The one I left upon a heap of corn
Which a brave miller in his boat had stored,
A better refuge than my breast forlorn:
  'Then through the wildness of this land abhorred
With this poor babe my steps I hither drew.—
To her I ask that pity thou afford.'
  No more she spake: but groans to silence grew,
And the end came: then my good father took
The child, and gave the poor corpse burial due:
  But first this very cloth on which I look
He from her neck unwound, that all might see

H 2

By token of what rank the babe partook.
And so henceforth the little maid with me
And with my brothers twain was nursed and reared,
Nor ever less than sister seemed to be,
Till lovely beauty in her face appeared,
And we were men: then love inflamed us all,
And broke our peace with jealousies unheard.
But soon our strife again to peace did fall:
For she the youngest for her bridegroom chose,
And took with him departure from our hall.
Unto those hills she passed that round us close,
Where she the Saracens to concord bent,
And lived in peace amid those heathen foes:
And with them both my other brother went."
Thus spake that knight upon the bloody plain:
And Mano answered: " To that argument
"Add this: thy other brother by me slain,
Since none but he rode with her to my spear:
And eke thy youngest brother dead, certain,
" By her whom thou hast leman: for by her
Was the other woman's husband stricken dead
From secret ambush in the hills, or e'er
" The battle chanced upon the mountain head,
Wherein I stood forth the deliverer
Of her by whom all is to ruin led.
" And to this woe exceeding add by her
Likewise thy foster-sister done to death:
And know that I, who to thine eyes appear,
" Am son of her who died upon the heath,
And brother of thy foster-sister so.
The compt between us sadly tallieth.
" Wherefore now fight we not: hence to her go,

Who brought this ruin both for thee and me.
Go not in love : go as an armed foe :
"Spare not ; but smite her for this misery.
Then, after that, our reckoning shall be made.—
I slew thy brother, as our sister she :
"And of my love by thee I am betrayed.
But older kindness sometimes may prevail :
(Thy father to my mother gave his aid) :
" If honour stand full satisfied, nor fail,
When ancient benefits with it be weighed,
Albeit these bring down the doubtful scale :
" In sleep, perchance, may enmity be laid."
  Then the knight bowed his head, and turned away.
But ere he parted, once more Mano said,
" Of him who was my father canst thou say :
Or else no knowledge hast, nor sign to bring ? "
The other answered, " Nought save this I may :
" That he of some high lineage did spring :
But of his rank or country and estate
I from my father never heard a thing."
  The other answered, " Truly of the great
Fair bounty have I in my life received.
The son of such a father fits my fate."
  So parted they : and, be it well believed,
The Italian knight rode to his death that day.
For travelling alone, in spirit grieved,
 Far from the Ungrians, who were fled away,
Unto his lodging lone he weened to ride,
Where the false woman, whom he cherished, lay.
 He found himself upon a country wide,
Travelling a road paven with stones full great,
Through which the long grass grew with lonely pride.

So went he, till the night grew very late,
And met with none : till last he saw a tomb,
Which by the roadside stood with ruined gate.
　Like a bastile it stood with spacious room
And rounded rampires high, which had been made
By the old pagans in the days of Rome :
　And evil spirits there their dwellings had.
He entered, since no better might be found,
Stabling his beast within the noisome shade ;
　And went to sleep lodged in the thick-walled mound.
But in the night (whether by secret ways
She issued, or by passage underground,
　Or by the fiends carried through cloudy haze ;
And whether knowing of his altered mind,
Or of his love grown weary, nothing says
　The history) she whom with purpose blind
He meant to slay, with bursting laughter woke
His sleep : certain she was of hellish kind :
　·And in the morning with his bones y-broke
Thus was he found by men who came that way,
Whose fearful ears gathered the words he spoke,
　Ere that he died : and thus that fiend did slay
Those brothers three, and Mano's sister dear :
And over Mano by her evil play
　Wove a dark web of wretchlessness and fear.

X.—THE CONTINUATION OF OUR JOURNEY.

NOW toward the Apennines our way we bent,
　Leaving the Lombards in tranquillity,
Unto Spoletum, whither we were sent,
　And Beneventum, where the war flamed high.

A POETICAL HISTORY.

Through the long forests, fens, dells, crags, and caves
Of that long back which bends through Italy,
   Where old Clitumnus drives his sacred waves,
Our journey lay: thence might our eyes survey
The sea, each shore of Italy that laves.
   But everywhere the land around us lay
Prostrate, and trampled by outlandish feet;
For, so in that, as now 't is in this day.
   The warring nations in those limits meet:
In gallies proud the Greek and Saracen
Upon the sea's broad back their strokes repeat,
   And join their war against the Lombard men,
In aid of whom the German marches slow
In heavy ranks: yea, e'en as now, so then.
   Against the Greek their solid force they throw,
But little boasts the German sword success
Against the walls and engines of that foe:
   For Greek and Saracen together press
The Latin empire from Apulia,
The Lombard limits growing daily less.
   But not yet, Bari, strength of Adria,
Hadst thou devoured those principalities,
Salernum, Beneventum, Capua.
            Thither our course: to join them as allies,
Adding the Norman to the Lombard power,
And make to cease by war war's miseries.
   Which as we sought, Mano from hour to hour
Like to himself appeared a leader great,
Whatever storm of peril nigh might lower.
   And in that time, touching those evils late
He spoke with me, who gave him full reply,
Admonishing of deeds unfortunate.

Albeit I feared him somewhat, yet was I
Faithful in that, the duty which I owed;
And won of him honour the more thereby.

Then, looking on me, presently he showed
A curious riddle song that he had made
Concerning those strange chances on our road:

Where in a doubtful manner was displayed,
And sadly told indeed a story true:
For this the song that he before me laid.

"I had a sister whom I never knew,
Because I saw her not, when I could know,
Albeit we shared the mother whom we slew.

I saw her not enough to know her so:
Nor, though she lived to be as old as I,
I saw her not in maiden garments low.

And yet unto my presence she drew nigh,
My hand was laid upon her golden hair,
But hand was granted not in hand to lie.

Ah, and my touch has pressed her unaware:
No foe was she, yet her I overthrew:
I spoiled her not, and yet her spoils I wear.

"And that poor sister, whom I never knew,
She had a brother who no brother was:
Which false-called brother into husband grew.

And both by one who caused me shame, alas,
That husband brother and herself were slain.

"I had a mother, who from me did pass:
A father, who no father was, certain.
One not my father father was to me,
My mother was not mine by mother's pain.

"A father then had I, third in degree:
A brother, and another, and another:

And brothers to my sister there were three ;—
Two, with the one that husband grew from brother :
But of them all not one that then we had
To us by blood was father, brother, mother.
 " Next, of those two that were by fortune sad
Left brothers of my sister, one I slew,
The other passed from me in menace clad.
 Now, when these chances I in thought pursue,
Thinking of what I had yet never had,
Dolour and pity bid my mind to rue,
But wrong is scarcely mixed with thinking sad."

XI.—HOW MANO MET WITH COUNT THUROLD,
DIANTHA'S FATHER.

HIGH-TOWERED Spoletum made we thus in march,
That spreads along the hills her gleaming wall :
And through that gate we entered, on whose arch
 Is written the defeat of Hannibal,
The town's old glory and enduring pride :
And there dwelt Thurold and his knights withal.
 Great was the joy that was on either side,
When there we met whom we to seek were come
Auxiliars in their fortune's wavering tide.
 A high man seemed the count, keen and blithe-
some,
And, as an old knight, straight and light of port,
Gay as an eagle in his mountain home.
 He made us welcome in a fitting sort ;
The father of the false Diantha he
Whom Mano carried to the Norman court.

"Fair son, for son indeed art thou to me,"
Thus he to Mano, "from an older day,
Not failing scion of a bending tree,
"I who first taught thee arms, and see thee pay
My quittance in the sword that thou dost bear
Against mine enemies, what shall I say?
"Joy bringest thou for woe, hope for despair
By thy return; and my brave family
By many noble sons dost thou repair,
"All who to join my banner come with thee:
Thou art my first-born of the sword; and these
Thy younger brethren: for one house are we,
"Whom warlike danger binds more fast than peace.
Now, lifted by this aid above dismay,
Soon shall we cause the Greekish foe to cease,
"And drive him hence from these fair realms away,
Though thick in every field his armed bands,
And far the cruel spoiler hunt his prey."
  Thus nobly spake he: and with joined hands,
Bade welcome to us all, and kindly cheer,
And into hall we came by his commands.
  That night was held a feast in high manner;
Where, as we sat, Sir Thurold presently
After Diantha asked, his daughter dear;
  To whom full sadly Mano made reply,
—"Sir, both to carry out and not fulfil
A purposed thing, into that case came I,
"Who bore your noble daughter by your will
To her old home, and there delivered her:
Whence either she by waywardness did steal,
"Or was conveyed by wicked ravisher:
Nor found again, though sought both far and wide."

Then sad that old knight grew with altered cheer:
And in that hour seemed hurt amidst his pride:
But with high bearing still no word he threw
Of grievousness in all that he replied:
Nay rather it appeared as if he grew
More gentle toward Sir Mano, knowing well
That to his power he faithful was and true:
The more, that he to extenuate nought did mell
Of that ill luck, nor of the time delayed
By him in Normandy beneath love's spell:
When he his musters slowly drew to aid,
And now was come but late with laggard powers:
All this the old man to oblivion bade.

  Man's love of man all other loves devours;
But the love of age to youth is wonderful:
The withered tree looks on the tree that flowers,
 Age from the eyes of youth fresh life doth pull.
For memory wakes therein the marvel owed
By age to youth, when age by time made null
Beholds strong youth still under life's huge load.

XII.—OF A VISION OF HELL, WHICH A MONK HAD.

OUT of this town there riseth a high hill,
 About whose sides live many anchorites
In cells cut in the rock with curious skill,
 And laid in terraces along the heights;
This holy hill with that where stands the town
The ancient Roman aqueduct unites;
 And passing o'er the vale her chain of stone,
Cuts it in two with line indelible;
A work right marvellous to gaze upon.

To one of those grave hermits there befell
A curious thing, whereof the fame was new
In our sojourn ; the which I here will tell.
    He found himself, when night had shed her dew,
In a long valley, narrow, deep, and straight,
Like that which lay all day beneath his view.
    On each hand mountains rose precipitate,
Whose tops for darkness he could nowise see,
Though wistful that high gloom to penetrate;
    And through this hollow, one, who seemed to be
Of calm and quiet mien, was leading him
In friendly converse and society:
    But whom he wist not: neither could he trim
Memory's spent torch to know what things were said,
Nor about what, in that long way and dim.
    But as the valley still before him spread,
He saw a line, that did the same divide
Across in halves : which made him feel great dread.
    For he beheld fire burning on one side
Unto the mountains from the midmost vale;
On the other, ice the empire did discide,
    Fed from the opposing hill with snow and hail.
So dreary was that haunt of fire and cold,
That nought on earth to equal might avail.
    Fire ended where began the frozen mould,
Both in extreme at their conjunction :
So close were they, no severance might be told :
    No thinnest line of separation,
Like that which is by painter drawn to part
One colour in his piece from other one,
    So fine as that which held these realms apart.
And through the vale the souls of men in pain

From one to the other side did leap and dart,
  From heat to cold, from cold to heat again :
And not an instant through their anguish great
In either element might they remain.
  So great the multitude thus tossed by fate,
That as a mist they seemed in the dark air.
  No shrimper, who at half-tide takes his freight,
  When high his pole-net seaward he doth bear,
Ever beheld so thick a swarm to leap
Out of the brine on evening still and fair,
  Waking a mist mile-long 'twixt shore and deep.
    Now while his mind was filled with ruth and fear,
And with great horror stood his eyeballs steep,
  Deeming that hell before him did appear,
And souls in torment tossed from brink to brink :
Upon him looked the one who set him there,
  And said : " This is not hell, as thou dost think,
Neither those torments of the cold and heat
Are those wherewith the damned wail and shrink."
  And therewith from that place he turned his feet ;
And sometime on they walked, the while this man
In aguish shuddering did the effect repeat:
  Such spasms of horror through his body ran,
Walking with stumbling, and with glazed eyes
Whither he knew not led, ghastly and wan.
  Then said the other: " In those agonies
No more than hell's beginning know : behold,
The doom of hell itself is otherwise."
  Therewith he drew aside his vesture's fold,
And showed his heart : than fire more hot it burned
One half : the rest was ice than ice more cold.
  A moment showed he this : and then he turned,

And in his going all the vision went:
And he, who in his mind these things discerned,
Came to himself with long astonishment.

XIII.—OF THE WAR.

TILL summer's drought had laid the streams all low,
　　Shrunken beneath their channel stones that lay,
Their white beds vainly thirsting for the flow
　　Which washed them in the spring with foaming play,
Clothing with water what they stripped to the bone
Of earth, and now uncovered did betray,
　　Lurking beneath their strewage, scarcely shown,
Like bodies deep in graves, whose bones remain,
And which survive in skeletons alone:
　　Till bitter winter came with clouds and rain,
Spreading his grim wing o'er the faint-laid earth,
And filled again with life each secret vein
　　That suffered drouth lest man should suffer dearth,
And with pure blood fed summer at the root:—
Till time's great march had so far issued forth,
　　The Normans held the forest-hidden foot
Of ancient Apennine, whence sulphurous Nar
Westward his white and furious stream doth shoot.
　　They in fierce battles drove their foemen far
Along the Apulian lands, across those streams
Which meet the Adrian waves with ceaseless war.
　　Thurold and Mano shone with equal beams,
And in those wintry battles sowed the corn
Of plenteous peace in summer's golden gleams.
　　Ah, but the wretched soil, which should have borne
That blessed harvest, by the heavy rain

Of conflict from the very rocks was torn.
Too thin the soil such harrowing to sustain.
But for a time was respite : and the foe
Most part in Bari did himself contain,
Warned from the field by constant overthrow.
But all that war in other histories
Is written, where its fame all men may know;
Wherefore I leave it now : for mine it is
To follow Mano to his destined end,
More than of storied glory that was his
In a redoubled roll to comprehend.

END OF BOOK II.

BOOK III.

BOOK III.

I.—HOW MANO WENT TO ROME.

HAPPY the man who so hath Fortune tried
That likewise he her poor relation knows:
To whom both much is given and denied:
 To riches and to poverty he owes
An equal debt: of both he makes acquist,
And moderate in all his mind he shows.
 But ill befalls the man who hath not missed
Aught of his heart's desires, in plenty nursed:
For evil things he knows not to resist:
 And, aiding their assault, himself is worst
Against himself, with self-destructive rage.
But states are with another evil cursed,
 For falling into luxury with age,
They burst in tumults, swollen with bloody shame,
Which old exploits aggrieve and not assuage.
 Past temperance doth the present feast inflame;
Past grandeur like too heavy armour weighs:
Great without virtue is an evil name.
  Rome, that was this world's head in ancient days,
Proud, lustrous, bloody, glorious witch and queen,
Beheld by all the nations with amaze,

The marble city, the hills of golden sheen,
Being fallen now into her shameless age,
With limy ruin overspread her scene.
 Old Tiber wound through her waste heritage:
Of bygone fame her virtue was the spoil:
Who seemed best was the worst bird in her cage;—
 That Vicar, who should others' sins assoil,
The Pope upon his throne, blazing with gold
And purple, which his monstrous crimes did soil,
 Bursting with pride, in ignorance thickly rolled,
Void both of knowledge and of charity,
Seemed the last plague poured on the world grown old:
 He seemed the very Antichrist to be,
Or else a statue and an idol dumb,
In God's own temple sitting wickedly.
 Thus Gerbert, ere his day of power was come,
Had oftentimes in fearless words declared
In Rheims before the Council, touching Rome:
 Gerbert, who now was pope: and now who dared
To notify his reign by acts severe
Against the abused time, and change prepared:
 But when he gan the sanctuary to clear,
He was by death prevented in strange way:
And impious vice her front again gan rear.
 Scarce had he gained that seat for his brief stay,
And straightway his stern rule commenced then,
When Mano reached that city of high sway,
 Turning his course westward from east again,
To meet his former friend and master there,
After those wars 'gainst Greek and Saracen.
 And with him good Sir Thurold did repair
From mountainous Spoletum through the vales

Which sink to Tiber's channel winding fair.
With them were others more: but me the gales
Of Fortune wafted not to Tiber's shore:
Sickness withheld: close furled were my sails.
And whilst I was delayed in trouble sore,
Mano and Thurold with great Gerbert met,
And made such joy that never might be more:
For Mano seemed the grievance to forget
Of Blanche's marriage, nor the part therein
Which Gerbert bore to hold in memory yet.
And Gerbert saw his cause in arms begin
To prosper, and to issue toward success
The plans that stood his spacious mind within:
Alas, full soon the chance must be to express
Which that restored friendship broke again,
And of their counsels made unhappiness.
Sir Mano honest was, as I maintain,
Even in that thing which brought to him his fall:
But honesty in fight with fate is vain.
Him, howso, whom so lately with the pall
Now with that pluvial he saw magnified,
Which habits him who is the head of all,
Well pleased was he: and Gerbert bade him ride
At his right hand unto the Lateran,
Showing him all the mighty city's pride.
Then came the nobles, and the people ran
To hail the knights who had wrought victory:
The Præfect there, and every high-placed man,
Who bore the signs of Roman majesty,
The Consuls, the Decarchons: through the town
They marched all in a royal pageantry:
So that this light of honour and renown

Brightest of all it shone that Mano saw :
The occasion of his friend gave him the crown,
And the drawn lot seemed the like lot to draw.

II.—WHAT HAPPENED IN ROME: THAT MANO CAME
IN DANGER OF A FALL.

BUT with no longer date than doth make green
    The lingering wintry ash among the trees,
This favouring promise of the time was seen
    Mid lowering clouds to mourn its own decease.
The blowing buds, put forth with rein so free,
Fell from the branch by angry destinies,
    And severed honour from the rooted tree,
Which still endured, and ready stood to bear,
Though each new birth still fell to fate's decree.
        Sir Mano, living in that city fair,
That head of earth, and empire's lofty seat,
Beheld what strangest things were mingled there :
    For opposites within the same may meet :
And where religion held her sovereign throne,
There in her shade lay murder and deceit :
    O'er rapine vile was saintly order thrown,
And evil deeds were wrapped in priestly fold.
The pictured walls, the images of stone,
    Showing the acts of saints and martyrs old,
Were by apostates from apostles shamed,
Who in the temple's precinct bought and sold.
    And albeit Gerbert, now Sylvester named,
Wrought sore those dark abuses to abate,
Yet hardly this French pope his own reclaimed
    Among those creatures of an earlier date :

Fell passions seethed around his trembling throne
And all his steps were marked by secret hate.
  The sight of these things made Sir Mano groan
With troubled wonder that in holiest place
Impiety and fraud were highest flown :
  And while he fed his heart on foul disgrace,
A thing befell, which in the sequel cast
The cloud of fate on fortune's budding grace,
  And drove him from that land, as from the last.
But first, regard herein, I you require,
The destiny exact that him o'ercast.
  A man in sin may satisfy desire,
But pay no forfeit, and forgiven be,
If fate so will, that gives to all her hire.
  This Mano found, ye may full well agree,
When folly he committed by the way,
And yet lost not the name of piety.
  A man may mean the best to do and say,
But by the best be humbled and depressed,
And by the best work best his own decay :
  Because the best may like the worst be dressed,
If fate, mocking the best, her fraud apply
By his own best to slay who means the best.
  This other horn of fate, now lifted high,
Likewise Sir Mano felt, when that befell
Which sudden was, and came full dangerously.
  When now, being sad in thought, and meaning well,
To ill for good his deeds by all were bent;
And in misprision prized by fatal spell.
  Yea, who should most have known his good intent,
And in whose grace he sought the most to abound,
That man the most his trouble did augment.

But speak no more of fate and fatal wound:
Say rather that transgression pays the price,
In whatsoever coin the same be found.
  To mark the extremes of fate be not o'er-nice:
Whether of evil seeming good unshent,
Or good ill-seeming smitten in a trice.
  For if the sinner fail of punishment,
And then in doing well be ill apaid,
This of the other is equivalent,
  And may be consequent, howso delayed.—
Nor say, the fool may everything commit,
And ne'er with him a reckoning be made:
  But if the good from goodness start one whit,
Down is he smitten by a thousand woes:
A thousand justices in judgment sit,
  A thousand lictors deal most righteous blows.—
Nor add that if the good deserve no blame,
But do a thing that like to evil shows,
Such as fools daily do, it ends the same.

III.—THE STORY OF LAURENTIUS AND HIS CHILDREN.

TO tell then by what snare stern Fate o'ercast
  Sir Mano's fortunes: On a certain day
Into his lodging secretly there passed
  A damsel fair, who piteously gan pray,
And knelt to him, her mistress dear to aid:
" For if thou aid her not, none other may,
  None in this evil place," the damsel said,
" Of fair renown for actions good and brave,
Worthy to hear the prayer that I have prayed.
  Hear therefore thou, and grant the boon I crave

Albeit therein such heart of peril lie
That thou mayest shun it, if thou fear the grave.
   A man there lives in power and station high,
Who sometime wrought a dismal deed in Rome,
The fame of which lurks in obscurity :
   For horrors here on horrors quickly come,
Like raindrops, which on one another pelt,
Obliterating each the other's room.
   " This man, when bold Crescentius lately dealt
His blow against the Emperor, but thereby
Wrought his own fall, and bitter vengeance felt,—
   This man was set in judgment's office high
By the triumphant Germans : but the place
Where he heard justice was a murderous sty.
   They of the insurrection in his face
Saw ready written executioners,
Whips, irons, dungeons, and refused grace.
   " Among the rest who thus in case adverse
Were cast, a certain senator was found,
Her sire to whom thy handmaid ministers.—
   Noble Laurentius stood before him bound
With his two sons, who in the attempt had shared,
Which first upraised, then dashed our hopes to ground.
   He for Rome's safety now his own despaired,
And was commanded to the gibbet straight,
And his two sons in equal ruin paired ;
   When, lo ! his daughter flung her piteous weight
Before the tyrant's throne, and clasped his knees
With frantic supplication 'gainst their fate.
   " The ruthless man at first but bade her cease,
And with rude push of hands her prayer denied,
Threatening to add her sentence unto these :

When suddenly with changed thought he cried
To stay the deed of death : and thereto sent
Messengers to that end, who swiftly hied.
    For her fair face with tender ravishment
Right suddenly transformed him, as he gazed,
And unto mercy turned his cruel bent.
    His own obduracy the wretch amazed :
Alas! had he to justice sooner given
What now to lust, for cursed he had been praised.
    For great Laurentius' soul was gone to heaven
Ere the reprieve came nigh : his sons alone
Were rescued, who to dungeon back were driven.
    " Then of her father's death such bitter moan
She made, and held his slayer in such hate
As almost turned to fear his hope new-blown :
    His hope new blown, which feared to demonstrate
Its evil tenor to that sorrow true :
He only said, ' Let it thy rage abate
    ' That if my erring voice thy father slew,
Thy brothers by my gift in life remain.'
Nor more that day did he his suit pursue.
    " But in short space his thoughts returned again ;
And he assayed my lady day by day,
To her entombed heart seeking in vain.
    Anon (false love is hasty, true can stay
For altered mind) one rage another woke,
And both her brethren threatened he to slay :
    And, as she still disdained his greedy yoke,
Holding her constant mind by threats unbent,
His vengeful arm let fall indeed the stroke.
    Her elder brother to the scaffold went ;
And since he finds his suit no better crowned,

He threatens what remains of punishment:
Now he prepares the last, the heaviest wound,
Renewing execution on her fere,
The truest gentleman that is on ground,
The last remaining, and to her most dear."

IV.—MANO UNDERTAKES THE VENGEANCE OF LAURENTIUS'S DAUGHTER.

"TOUCHING the matter of Crescentius,
Who made revolt against the Emperor,"
Mano replied, " Rumour hath reached to us.
For twice he strove to shut the Roman door
Against the Germans: and twice strove in vain.
Once, when he aimed the city to restore
Under the Greeks, in the first Otho's reign:
And for that turn he suffered banishment,
But afterwards essayed the same again:
Thinking, the Emperor then being resident
With but small force in Rome, to take him so:
And only chance frustrated his intent:
Whereon being driven to Saint Angelo
By the stout German power, there he sustained
Long time both siege and famine: till, brought low,
To one he yielded who no mercy deigned."
—" Yea," said the woman, " and to those who shared
His bold attempt dire punishments remained:
For him indeed 'twas bitter, when he dared
Under consent of the Emperor appear
Amid the Saxon tents, whither he fared.—
By stealth he left his tower, and ventured near,
Clad in blue mantle, and with covered head

And to the Emperor came with suppliant prayer.
But cruel taunts his faith dishonoured.
'Now is the Saxon tent the entertainer,'
(With visage sour the third young Otho said,)
'Of him that was of emperors constrainer,
Prince of the Romans, and the city's head,
Giver of laws, and of new popes ordainer.'—
Hard was it thus to be to scaffold led:
But harder was the fate reserved for those
Who followed him: more sore were they bested.
Thus, John Philagathus, whom pope he chose,
Sometime of Piacenza archbishop,
Was great in wealth before these troubles rose:
But being taken as usurping pope,
The cruel conqueror robbed him of tongue,
Cut off his nose, and both his ears did crop,
And him thus maimed into a dungeon flung,
Where he was found by Nilus his old friend,
Nilus the Eremite, whom fame hath sung:
To whom full many unto this season wend
To find the future from his augury.—
He, grieving much to see fulfilled the end
Which he had promised, left his covert shy,
And, viewing how the maimed wretch was laid,
Rebuked the emperor with authority,
And his great cruelty did so upbraid
With zeal from heaven, that insolence was quelled,
And for the future base revenge seemed stayed.
Alas! a moment more the effect dispelled
Of holy age upon remorseless youth:
And soon that barbarous minister prevailed
Who holds us all in fear, who knows not ruth,

He against whom I now invoke thy aid,
If thou art brave, and lovest gentle truth."
  Then Mano said, " This scarce should be essayed
By any man, and last of all by me.
For know that he who lately Pope is made
 In place of him who bore this cruelty,
Gerbert, is my great master, whom I hold
Above all men in honour's highest gre.
 He in the Papal number was enrolled
By him who slew John and Crescentius,
Otho the third, his pupil young and bold.
 Wherefore for me to stir is perilous,
Since Gerbert now is mingled verily
With the forceful Cæsar fierce and tyrannous.
 But yet his virtue wills not villany.
Say therefore thou what way I may assist
To your desires, and what I can will I."
  Then said the damsel, " Even so as I wist
I find thy worth: know therefore what we find:
(Now sinking day the darkness doth enlist,
 And bids to aid our part): it is our mind
To bid to banquet that unhonoured guest,
Whom cruelty made fell, false love made kind:
 There shall he meet my lady richly dressed,
Whose face, no more in horror lifted up,
Shall smile on him, and bid him to the fest.
 Then, when he hopes that he in joy shall sup,
(Such life such fate deserves) we have in plot
To work his death by sword or poisoned cup.
 But women's arms are weak, their hands do not
According to the counsel of their heart,
Or changed hearts make their purposes forgot:

Therefore I thought to make thee of our part,
And trust to thee this execution drear,
Who hast a mind that terror cannot start.
   And now, behold! the hour is drawing near:
The trap is set: the strong and hungry prey
Comes to the bait, which he shall never tear,
Ere the sprung spring shall dash him down.   Away!"

V.—THE ADVENTURE PURSUED.

HEREAT with haste Sir Mano took his sword,
   And through the Lateran garden they two sped.
Like the tightening and the loosening of a cord,
   Whereby a barge is up the river led,
The maiden's hand in his still touched palm
Drew him with fierceness as she onward fled:
   Till for their rushing there was total calm:
And passing through a doorway they were hid
In a dark place, suffused with scents of balm.
   The may laid hand upon a shutter-lid:
"Behold, and slay the monster:" saying so
The noiseless shutter back in groove she slid,
   And showed the room beyond in light: when, lo!
Instead of some grim-visaged cruel man,
And woman in great horror shrinking low,
   Or towering high with face by hate drawn wan,
A beautiful young man was there espied
Kneeling before the feet of a woman,
   Whose face of beauty o'er him bent soft-eyed:
A rich feast spread, sweet burning scents and wine
Seemed ready, as for bridegroom left with bride.
   At sight of which Mano withdrew his eyne:

But, "In and slay him now," the damsel cried,
" Even as the butcher slays a fatted swine."
 Even as she spoke, there came from the other side
Of that fair room a groan of misery :
A window dropped, and in with hasty stride
 A young man walked, and a drawn sword held he :
Whereat the other leaped upon his feet.
" Ah, wretch ! that hast beguiled my love from me,"
 The new man said, " by fraud and cursed deceit ! "
And quick they joined in fight with deadly din.
But he, that had been kneeling, with such heat
 Pressed on the other, that with weapon thin
Full soon he lanced his heart : nay, rather seemed
That other to his death to strive to win,
 So soon he fell, so quick his life-blood streamed.
Then cried the woman to the conqueror,
" Thou wretch ! with whom in dotage I have dreamed
 " For one dead moment, thinking thee no more
My father's and my brother's murderer,
Know that I bade thee enter by this door
 " Not for love's joys, but death's revenges drear.
And if thy fair looks and false constancy
Wrought me to seem to grant thee thy love-prayer,
 " To save my living brother, lo, I see
The effect thereof in this new added blood.
Forgive me, father, brothers ! forgive me
 " Lorenzo, proved by death a lover good,
Whom I have sent to death : ah, for that death
Thus Constance puts away her womanhood."
   Hereat with stabbing knife and hissing breath
On him she flies ; who keeps her well at bay,
And turneth with his sword, and parryeth.

All which was done more quick than words can say,
And Mano long before the last word here
Was in the midst, and mingled with the fray:
  He sought that man; who, stout and void of fear,
Held him full long; and up and down they fought,
And many cruel wounds between them were:
  But at the last the man to ground was brought:
Yet thence again, when Mano nearer drew,
Springing, that lady for a shield upcaught;
  Who, being swung on high between the two,
Cried, "Smite and spare not, even though I die."
But Mano, her avoiding, smote him through,
  And with his own stroke prone on earth did lie.
Senseless through bleeding wounds: so lay those three
By one another in that tragedy.
  But he who first had fallen, difficultly
Forced his still grasping hands from the waist to the throat
Of that fair woman, that his agony
  Might be her strangling: and the same, I wot,
Had happened soon enough, but that the may
Who brought Sir Mano, his hands asunder smote:
Then like a snake uncurled in death he lay.

VI.—HOW MANO WAS BANISHED BY GERBERT.

WHEN death hath done his part, and in his tomb
    Shut up the world, the judgment shall begin.
Mano, awaking as from death, found doom
  And judgment waiting him, as if for sin,
Instead of joy of dear-bought victory.
For rising dizzily that room within,
  Where stood the lady and the may thereby,

(The lady who had brought him back to life,
Being herself saved through his courage high,
 The may who first had drawn him to the strife,
Then staunched his bleeding wounds with healing skill)
Behold, amid the gloom of shadows rife,
 Grave forms he sees, which half the chamber fill,
And fix upon him their regardful eyes :
First among whom, and ominous of ill,
 Gerbert himself he gins to recognise ;
Round whom his ministers in station stand,
All summoned by the clash, the groans and cries.—
 He now Sir Mano sternly bore in hand,
And, as the ruler over all supreme,
The cause of quarrel asked with grim demand.
           Then those two women all the tale to him
Rehearsed from first to last with eager tongue,
Their woes that like a sea of blood did swim ;
 And told how seeking vengeance on great wrong,
They bade that knight become the instrument
Of death on him who there lay dead along.
 All which was heard with visage still unbent
By Gerbert, and in silence drear and cold,
Such silence as the tale to distance sent,
 And severed it from those by whom 'twas told :
Until incredible as phantasy
E'en to themselves appeared their sufferings old,
 And their new deed as done but wickedly.—
Such was the effect of silence long and drear,
More terrible than closest scrutiny.
 Then questioned he, redoubling thus their fear;
And though with very truth they made reply,
In no wise gained they way into his ear :

K

Anon he waved his hand, as putting by
Their story, and pronounced his stern award.
—— " Ye, even as yourselves do testify
" Have slain a man by treachery at board,
Of him alleging wrongs inordinate,
Which drew upon him your unsparing sword.
 " Have ye approached to justice to delate
One of those injuries that ye complain,
Seeking the open order of the state?
" Not so: I know not aught that now ye feign:
Nor, were it so, would there from thence ensue
The extenuation of a murder plain.
" But this I know, that by a sentence true
Thy father died, who seconded the raid
Of bold Crescentius and his desperate crew:
" And after him thy brother forfeit paid:
The third, thy other brother, living still,
By mercy respited, in bonds is laid.
" Now in return ye have not spared to kill
The judge, who spared your side the extremest cost,
Through two attackers brought with wicked skill.
" I therefore judge your lives in forfeit lost
To violated law for murderous deed,
Though of strict right I waive the uttermost:
" For judgment's arrow mercy's point shall lead;
Nor used is all the law's severity,
If on you both for sentence stand decreed
 The cloister's dimness, to that day ye die."
—— " Then praised be thou, my soul's mediciner!
I would not otherwise, nor doom deny:
 " I would not purge the thick wax of thine ear,
Nor scale thine eyes to justice," loud did cry

That lady blooming in her sweetest year.
" Nothing was left to me except to die
Beside my lover fallen from life's delight;
But thou hast given me life in misery."
  Then hand in hand those two passed out of sight,
Thrust by the guards, to meet their life-long doom:
And Mano there was left in bloody plight.
  To whom thus Gerbert spake: while from the gloom
Of his deep presence steadfastness and pain
In revolution, like moved light, did come:
" Thou too, in whom I trusted, I am fain
To meet thee now with sorrow, and rebuke:
For thou hast broken service with loose rein,
  " Dishonouring me, to whom thou most shouldst look,
In my high office: death is thine by right,
Who hast to death thy fellow servant struck.
  " Oh, Mano, camest thou like a thief by night,
And, with another joined, settedst thy steel
Against a single man in unfair fight?
  " Not so, not so; this I both know and feel:
But thou hast taken taint: and this time first
Thy new-found wounds I call not honour's seal.
  " I say not that the best becomes the worst
In thee, though thee the best of all I know
That have with me the road of days traversed:
  " But hence thou must from out this city go."
—Then Mano, laughing loudly, cried, " A friend!
I have a friend to hold in weal or woe!
  " A man to be right faithful to the end!
In judgment undeceived, and knowing good
Where others evil falsely apprehend!
  " Unerring as the hands upon the Rood

That measured the two thieves! I had a friend
Who was aforetime fair and mild of mood :
 "Faithful was he to many to the end :
Of judgment clear : in many knowing good
Where others sought but ill to apprehend :
 "For will and deed he rightly understood.—
Only in me this Vicar of God's throne
No mirror showed of perfect rectitude."

  Then Gerbert sternly said, "If there be one
Trusted for worth, who less than worth is found
In high designs, there is one way alone :
 "His former service falls not to the ground,
But he has run his length : yet to upbraid
Needs not, to break old friendship with such wound."

  Then Mano laughed again, and fiercely said,
"Servant of servants, if by villany
In combat I took odds, being afraid,"—
—"I said not so," said Gerbert—"Nay, then I
Of all that thou mayest think, put by the rest;
And thy deep reasons seek not curiously."

  Thus with a high look locked he in his breast
Reproach, defiance, anger ; all but pride :
Which only from some taunt was not repressed.

  And certainly pope Gerbert on his side
Was neither friend nor judge : betwixt the two
From friendship failed he, justice to o'erride.

 Friendship against appearance would be true,
Justice would search a cause from end to end ;
The one not look, the other all things view.

 But the half pardon but insults the friend
Whom the half sentence wrongs : wholly to quit,
Or not at all, doth judgment's seat commend.

This fault did Gerbert in that hour commit,
When he, misjudging, balanced judgment's sway
With other thought in his deep working wit.
And thus of policy he wrought decay,
When Mano now, unlet by any one,
Out of the fatal chamber took his way,
Destined no more to prop the Roman throne.

VII.—WHAT LED GERBERT TO MISJUDGE MANO.

WHEN two fair ships that in one road are moored
The wave uplifts, their dipping hulls incline
This way and that together: then restored
To calm, together sleep above the brine.
Their play, their peace alike would make it seem
That the same suns upon their course must shine.
But presently one seeks the ocean stream,
At anchor still the other's governance :
Or both sail diverse in an hour supreme.
So they who meet by friendship's sacred chance
Would join their courses, and together speed,
Finding no cause of sudden severance :
But Fate's deep kedge lies in life's watery breade,
Life's bellying sail is spread to destiny,
From one another those paired barks recede.
Gerbert with Mano held society,
And loved him much, and seemed to hold him fast,
Making him main to all his counsels high.
Greater the marvel therefore, when he cast
On pretext false his helper from his side,
And struck him without justice at the last.

But Mano, being demanded, still replied
That Gerbert wrought by politic intent,
Which weighed with him above all things beside :
   That therefore was the sentence banishment,
(To rid him thence,) and not such penalty
By which, if he had erred, he might repent :
   Whence, being no more in trust, to magnify
The matter, and engrieve by words, were vain,
And better to depart indifferently.

   But I, against him arguing, would maintain
That Gerbert in this deed was worse to see
Than his renown, of low and captious strain.
   For sometimes men that are of high degree
Carry not gentle thought in lordly vest ;
And, in their office, of offence are free.
   Such men, perchance, from whom they have oppressed
Receiving some strong lesson, presently
Become of mien more courteous toward the rest.
   But still the original baseness deep doth lie
Within them : and their false conclusion is,
That since to all they now use courtesy,
   And with one man alone have fallen from this,
Therefore the right has been with them alway :
The fault, before and in the strife, was his.

   I thought that Gerbert thus had gone astray
In Mano, and would not again repeat
For others what he sought to do and say :
   But that he ne'er would from that wrong retreat,
Being puffed and swollen beyond all charity,
Though cautious grown, upon his lofty seat.
   But in that argument unsound was I :
For Gerbert was no churl of vulgar mind

Upraised by fortune's wheel to prelacy.
Yet something was there in him that inclined
The balance against Mano in that day,
As they who end this history shall find :
For ere from Normandy he took his way,
He had secretly freed Mano from the vow
Which bound him service to the Church to pay.
 Wherefore perchance less unregardful now,
When he repelled his friend so utterly
To all men's seeming, was in truth the blow.
 Well might he deem that he to Normandy
Would thence return : and there Joanna lay,
His loving friend, in dreary nunnery.
 This quittance Mano knew not, when his stay
Broke in the waters whither it was cast,
And life's new breeze blew through his anchorage bay :
 But whispers rose, which o'er the trembling vast
Invited him, and caused him not to mourn
While his brave vessel clothed her rocking mast.
 Unto past cheer his busy mind gan turn :
Spent fires must die : new fuel verily
Wakes an old fire in other wise to burn.
 But if those two had still kept company,
Neither so short had been Sylvester's date,
Nor to such end reached the knight's tragedy.
But other drafts were in the book of fate.

VIII.—MANO PARTS FROM THUROLD, BUT NOT FROM FERGANT.

OLD Thurold, heavy-hearted at this case
From Rome with Mano to Spoletum rode,
And more than he enraged with his disgrace,
At evening gained with him my poor abode,
Wherein with sickness sharp I lay immured :
Where, when the old knight had all that history showed,
With glittering eyes obedience he abjured
Thenceforth to Gerbert; deeming it foul wrong
That had to his dear Mano shame procured.
—" Certes the French pope speaks with German tongue
Quoth he, "and wary is he, as it seems :
And such the man must be who goes along
" The priestly path that leads to Rome from Rheims :
Hostile to Normans must such man be found ;
Yet may he not be safe, as now he deems,
" Doing despite to us upon God's ground."
But Mano said, " In silence it is best
To feel the smarting of a cureless wound.
" For not with Gerbert can I ease my breast
In open quarrel and plain enmity.
Nor would past friendship from remembrance wrest :
" For know (if I here separate from thee),
That to have lost his fellowship is grief
Beyond the reach of wrathful mind to me ;
" To me, perhaps to him : and this mischief
Can never be recured ; now hence must I
My noble father, be I loth or lief :
" Nor doubt I where my voyage next must lie ;

For now the thought of thy deceived trust
Comes to me, guiding whither I should hie.
" I go to seek thy daughter, as is just,
Diantha, whom from Italy I led,
Who fled the Norman court through evil lust,
" As to our bitter scorn by all is said.
Thou blamest not my doing in that case,
But mine it is to go, most honoured head,
" To find what may be left against disgrace."
   Then they shook hands : and Thurold one word
    spake,
Turning away his high but fallen face :
" Son, thou hast wrung my heart before it break."
But Mano turned to go. Then from my chair
Rose I, and cried, " I go with thee for make,
" And still with thee by grace of God will fare,
Whither thou goest : and from land to land
What lot to thee be cast, the same to share."
 Then Mano smiled, and gave to me his hand,
Saying, " To have thee with me betters me
More than much else in this my waniand,
" Did but thy body with thy mind agree."
 —" My sickness is of mind : weary am I
To see the working of man's misery,
" And of this sickness sore if I should die,
Fain would I die at home in my own land ;
Nor wonder thou that I with thee would fly.
" For now the end of all things is at hand :
The Antichrist is come, who comes before ;
Then of the just the graves shall empty stand,
 " And last the General Judgment opens door."
Thus answered I, feeling full near to death,

In haste to leave the Babylonian shore,
  Deeming the earth then drawing her last breath.
Ah, I live still; and still the Antichrist
Reigns in the world, not passing underneath:
And still the dead sleep on in sealed cist.

END OF BOOK III.

BOOK IV.

BOOK IV.

I.—HOW MANO AND FERGANT RETURNED TO NORMANDY.

LIKE to the rising of the morning ray,
Albeit arisen on ruin, waste and wreck,
When storm has happened since the last sunk day,
So can the soul herself with brightness deck,
When new-found resolution bears her on,
And bids her not of broken hopes to reck :
So can she make to shine the beam that shone
On works that perished in a night of woe,
On waste of toil, on wreck of promise gone.
  Thus was it found, when we began to go
In homeward voyage our remeasured road
By river, plain, or hill, or valley low
 Which we had passed before : not now they showed
Their former face, the radiance that they wore,
The light by hope and enterprise bestowed.
 But when we came beyond the Italian shore
Into the Alps, the abrupt of icy cold,
Then Manó in his face new purpose bore;
 As if that late distress were now of old,
Or put to distance in the deeps of heart,
And to life's eye new solace were unrolled.

But I the while grew sadder on my part,
Foreboding more the nearer home we drew
Through all the realms that Burgundy dispart.
　And when to Normandy our travel grew,
That land which from old misery knew I,
But he from better memory only knew,
　Then hope more fully lit his inward eye;
And there at length we rested from our way,
And fixed ourselves in a fair hostelry.
　Then he bethought him of the prouder day
When he for Blanche the Fair had burned and sighed,
Who for Giroie had flung his love away:
　Of her much thought he and her glorious pride,
But of Joanna more, her sister dear,
Who now in cloister's strictness did abide.
The name of her full often did I hear
Burst from his lips with groanings miserable
Of pity, of love, and of distracted cheer.
　" Ah, couldst thou know, poor dove, how hard a
　　spell
Of heart-ache in my breast is kept for thee,
Sure holiness would comfort thee not well:
　" Thou, with whom once I joyed, thou who to me
Alone in life hast given that blessedness
Which but they know who love exceedingly:
　" Couldst thou know all, heaven might content thee less."
Thus would he say: or else in manner wild,
　" Was thy sweet banquet spread, thou gentleness,
　" Which wanted still thy guest, oh loveliest child!
Ah, now to me are many thoughts grown clear,
Which then I knew not, being but beguiled,
　" Yea, fooled perchance by him whom I held dear.

But now, albeit in a day too late,
To thy still dwelling am I drawing near."
　　Thus ever on the road he held debate,
Within his mind, suspicious, it might be,
Of Gerbert's counsel of unhappy fate,
　　Who kept Joanna's love in secrecy,
Whenas the same she did to him confess
Ere Mano took the way to Italy.
　　For love may kindle love, though late not less;
And kindled love, of whatso bars his way,
All secret though it be, is keen to guess.
　　　Then in the hostelry wherein we lay,
It came into my mind that not far thence
Stood Blanche's gard, the castle high and gay,
　　Where with Giroie she kept her residence,
And, filled with mighty wealth, her high-towered seat
Above her manors rose in eminence.
　　Which thing to Mano when I gan repeat,
He answered, " Dread have I, hearing that name,
For great upon me is her power sweet :
　　"But not the less go we to seek the same,
As pilgrims both : and thou the words shalt speak,
But I shall keep in silence, fearing shame."
　　　This was agreed when the next day should break.

II.—OF A STRANGE DREAM WHICH CAME TO FERGANT.

NOW that same night I dreamed a curious dream.
　　There were two lovers, who did envy oft
The little rabbits feeding in the beam
　　Of moonlit woods: if but they might have doffed

The pains of human nature : then at last
They both resolved to change into those soft
  Quick-shadowed things : they did so ; and there passed
A pleasant time : then he was changed again
Into a bear-like monster dark and vast,
  And she into her native form was ta'en.
To her he came : but she from her away
Drave him full fast : and he in grief was fain
  To climb into a tree, while down she lay
Upon a bank below : then presently
He crept again toward her : but might not stay,
  So fiercely met she him : and with a sigh
He went away again : and thus once more
She met him, when the third time he drew nigh.

  Then to his tree he moved, perplexed sore,
And waited midst the leaves fallen and brown,
And far off watched her on the forest floor :
  Until she cried, "Sir knight, sir knight, come down."
He ran to her, and found her covered o'er
With yellow things, as is the rabbit town
  With that thick-swarming people, " Many an hour,"
Said she to him, " have I lain on my side
In endless pains : now therefore me devour."
  Whereat he wept, and would not : then she died :
And, lo, there was another monster grim
And terrible, who rose up by his side :
And him that monster slew. Such was this dream.

III.—HOW SIR MANO SAW BLANCHE THE FAIR AGAIN.

THE morrow, as the day began to clear,
　　We took our way along the country brown,
Far as that hill where stood the castle near.
　　Like pilgrims were we clad in hood and gown :—
Alas, we went to gain but dule and teen
From blowing on love's torch burnt wholly down.
　　The castle with close windows seemed, I ween,
Refusing Blanche to us with sad aspect,
And heaved his thick wall with denying screen.
　　But we our steps stayed not, nor purpose checked,
Ere thither we arrived, and passed the gate.
(So they who sail to rocks must needs be wrecked.)
　　Then in a chamber we were bidden wait
The coming of that lady sweet and rare,
Who was to him the bitterness of fate.
　　　　She came, nor she alone : her husband there
Came with her, step by step : and round his neck
Her arm was cast : in sooth she left him ne'er,
　　What time she talked with us : nor sought to check
Her fondness for him, deeming us to be
Religious men, of whom no need to reck.
　　Slow was her gait, thus led on tenderly;
Most noble was her face : yea, fairer now
Than when her beauty drew all men to see,
　　And o'er bold eyes made droop their eyelids low ;
But pale she was, albeit so sweet of face,
And plain it was to see by signs enow
　　That very soon a babe should be in place.
Pity and love pulled both our hearts, I ween,

L

At her behaviour and her gallant grace.
　　Never so fair was Blanche the Fair yet seen :
For transport and love's plenitude were shed
On her great loveliness with ray serene.
　　Then with pleased voice, as one who sees the thread
Of his own dream confirmed by wayside thing,
While still he walks with dreams, to us she said :
　　"Ye holy men, from Italy who bring
News of the Normans there, welcome are ye :
And that ye tarry in your journeying,
　　" And to this castle turn aside for me,
The cause is not unknown, and must be told
Before mine husband, what it seems to be.
　　" Ye are from that knight Mano, who of old
(For old is that which is of other day)
To that same land his armed course did hold :
　　" No other thing than this espy I may."
—" No other thing is true," I soon answered,
" By Mano bidden we have turned this way,
　　" To know of thee what tidings might be heard.
For thee he held for lady of his thought,
When here he stood : and thee in heart revered."
　　—" Then tell him, since by right thus much is sought
And granted, that thou sawest me," she said,
" In happiness, to which all else is nought,
　　" With this dear knight, with whom my days are led :
Tell him that thought of all the past is gone,
That this sweet present makes the past more dead ;
　　" Since every living moment liveth on
In the same joy which to the next it gives :
And this dear knight, this sweet and perfect one,

"Ordains that as my joy in him, his lives
In me: in each the other's joy alone:
Joy that with life increase of joy receives."
  While thus she spoke, still round his neck was thrown
Her long and heavy arm; nor ceased she
With his large head to play, whose short curls shone:
And ever on him leaned she lovingly,
Staying on him her body's tender weight.
And Sir Giroie failed nought of courtesy,
 And gave to us good looks and welcome great,
Though Mano held himself but dumb the while.
" Ye holy men," then she, " this happy state
 " Which ye be come to witness many a mile,
Report to him who sent you hitherward;
And, since ye go, heaven on your journey smile.
 " But bid him of our joy think nothing hard,
For noble heart sees other's joy content;
And he one day may meet his joy prepared,
 " His lover true, by God unto him sent:
Which is the only joy preserved to man."
  Then thus in parting words toward her I went.
" Lady, the man thou namest never wan
That gift of human fortune, nor may win.
But leave we him: he with fair star began,
 " And so may end, e'en as he did begin,
Without the aid of love's all-moving power,
Which oftest works but sorrow, pain, and sin."
  This said, of other converse in that hour
In courteous gentleness did much ensue,
While yet we tarried in that happy bower:
 And of Diantha and Joanna true

Somewhat that day we learned, which in right place
Shall be related and set forth to view.
  And therewith parted we : and face to face
Mano and Blanche the Fair met never more,
And she in childbirth died in no great space :
 Whom always her sad love lamented sore,
And from possession passed to vacancy :
 Whom this, her lover of a day before,
Unknown beheld unknowing silently.
So love, but not of him, brought her to end,
So passeth she out of this history.
  And now we took our leave, and made to wend
Out from the chamber on our backward road :
The fair white clouds above the woods did bend,
 And measured out round hills and valleys broad,
And the light sunbeam travelled with the cloud.
But dark was Mano's heart with anger's goad,
 And in the court he chafed in his dark shroud :
But if he had been known, full well I ween
No pity to his pain had she allowed :
 For where was yet the woman ever seen
Who pitied the distempers of the mind ?
He smote his hand against the iron keen
 Whose heavy bar her lordly gates confined,
And from the stroke some drops of blood there flowed :
She to such wound had shown herself more kind
 Than to his wounded mind she ever showed.—
Oh, ordered well, lest earthly creature steal
That highest love to creature never owed !
  And here I add that which de Montreuil
Told me long after of this interview,
When kindness had no favour to conceal :—

That all the while he well Sir Mano knew,
But seeing that he kept himself unshown,
Gave never sign, neither his covert drew,
To find if Mano guessed that he was known.

IV.—OF A DREAM THAT CAME TO SIR MANO.

NOW when we gained the road, a sudden pain
Shot through my breast, making me like to die;
And I perceived my sickness come again.
    Upon the knight I leaned full heavily,
Whilst he with gentleness and kindly cheer
Conveyed me back into the hostelry.
    No further might we then in voyage steer,
But there long time in forced harbour lay,
And still upon me grew that sickness drear.
    And of that evil time I have to say
That it was bringing in our parting hour,
Which found her place in no far distant day,
    When Mano was borne from me by the power
Of evil fate:—in sickness I was left,
And him did flames of destiny devour.
    But ere the day that I was so bereft,
There chanced another thing, which I shall tell,
To show that destiny cannot be wefte;
    And how fate sendeth her forecasting spell.—
It was a dream, wherein in changeful maze
He was with Gerbert mixed, that him befell:
    This he to me related in those days;
And this it was: Appeared that they two
Were in a road beyond the city ways,

When first the ground was strewn with lighter snow;
And as their way they held, discoursing deep,
They seemed to meet with many whom they knew;
But next they were alone : then night gan creep
Upon the pathway : and the wood grew dark
On either hand ; 'twas hard the path to keep.
  Then past them somewhat went, it seemed a spark,
Which back returned around them dancingly ;
And something drear therein did Mano mark.
It seemed to be that man of Italy,
Whom he had slain, and for that crime had left
The land of his unknown nativity.
  Then Gerbert held him strongly ; but he reft
The hold of Gerbert, and the form pursued,
Which went before, not looking right or left,
  And vanished lastly in the ancient wood—
Then turned he back, and on the presage ill
Of that strange sign they both in thought did brood ;
  But neither spake, for they were pacing still
A darksome road of trouble and affright,
Till they beheld a house beside a hill,
  That stood amid wild trees, and by dim light
Was spread a darksome field, in midst whereof
A strong horse stood, that seemed a dangerous sight.
  But Mano said, "Lord Gerbert, long enough
We go afoot : mount thou this good horse now,
Since thou art wearied by this voyage rough."
  Then Gerbert said, "With folly avisest thou
To ride such horse : and furthermore I warn
That thou ride not, lest danger thereof grow."
  But Mano seized the horse with stubborn scorn :
And thereupon from out the wicket gate

An old man came, and said, " Of woman born
" None ride the horse without a loss full great :
For he will bear thee far ; but it shall be
To thine own hurt." But he, " Withhold debate :
   For whitherso this horse will carry me,
Thither it is my mind to mount and ride,
Even to my hurt."—" The horse will carry thee
   Far thitherward," the aged man replied.
" Farewell, Lord Gerbert," Mano answered there ;
" Tarry thou here, whatever shall betide,
For on this road I promise far to fare."

V.—OF THE SAME.

FULL long he rode amid the darksome waste,
   And mightily the fierce horse bore him on :
So that like clouds, that by the wind are chased,
   The dark trees overhead sailed one by one :
But the horse sped, like rage his courage high,
Till a white river in the pathway shone,
   Whose chilly stream gave answer to the sky ;
The which he crossed, but met again full soon,
And whitherso he turned, the stream was nigh :
   Heading his course, it still lay whitely strewn,
Or brimming, murderous dark, from shore to shore,
Or dully silvered, as by clouded moon.
   But last the enraged waves, his path before,
Ran broadly forth, and cast a bloody glare,
As if their breast an angry meteor bore :
   And their rough-watered bulks did heave and flare
In hillocks yellow and red. The war-horse proud
Leaped onward, rushing through the fiery air ;

And down the steep bank toward the surface bowed,
While his fierce feet the coltsfoot leaves trod down,
Whose mighty growth served the rough stones to shroud.
　And Mano saw the waters flash and frown,
And plunge beside the image of a fire,
Which seemed the other element to crown.
　Then was the river gone, with sudden ire;
And left behind a maiden standing there,
Whose coming strange in mind he gan admire:
　But knowing her to be Diantha fair,
Resolved to not admire, because he found
That he thereof had always been aware:
　But held her by the hand: when from the ground
She seemed with shrieks to rise: and in his hand
Only white bones remained, which dropped around,
　　And with their ruin littered all the land.
　　　　Herewith he started from his evil sleep,
Holding the dream within his mind's command,
But troubled at the same with trouble deep.

VI.—HOW MANO PARTED FROM FERGANT.

OH, mind of man, whose thoughts with travel sore
　　Cannot arrive the ground where simple sense
In the beginning stood: thou, who the more
　Thou strivest in the sum of things immense,
The less achieving, seest that centre firm,
Where thou wouldst plant thy footing, to move thence
　Crumbling resolve itself from term to term,
And leave unsure the measure that remains:
Thou, taking thought, canst not thyself confirm.

Thou canst not from the incorporeal plains
Of the old atomic chaos separate
Thyself: not that contained from that contains.
Nothing canst thou by thought discriminate;
For all is one and one is all by thought,
And motion cannot be in nature's state.
  But by the senses winged, thou sett'st at nought
The halting intellect: and at a bound
Reachest thy ends, which else were never raught.
 Thy deeds and being thought would fain confound,
And call not possible : but thou dost live,
Nor knowest thyself by mockeries wrapped and wound.
 So great a might to thee the senses give.
But when, cut off from sense, in sleep sopite,
The soul, not sensible, but sensitive,
 Takes her own instruments, of finer might
Than eye or ear, though fashioned to the same
Of purpose, then she sees further than sight,
 Hears more than sound : then doth her skill acclaim
O'er moveless thought her wider victories:
Then, if she sport, she maketh better game,
 And boldly spreads the shows she doth devise :
Or if to heaviness her mood be bent,
Being perplexed or troubled anywise,
 More swiftly then by her the cloud is rent
Which bears the thundrous store of threatening fate :
For past and last future to her present.
  So to the coming evil gave the date
That dream predictive, which the noble knight
Told to my ears, and did the same debate.
 The heads of things to come in wavering light
Moved up and down therein, as on the wall

Beyond my bed the arras shook in sight;
And its inwoven heads did rise and fall
Above the wood-fire's smoke invisible,
Which made them quiver and grow dim withal.
 Sad grew my heart to hear what he did tell,
But sadder, when he said, "I must be gone:
Therefore, dear fellow, bid I thee farewell:
 "But have no fear, I shall return anon;
For, as it seems to me, I soon shall find
Diantha, whom our quest is set upon.
 "But this may be to hurt: for to my mind
The thing that I have met seems verily
To show success to us, with harm behind."
 Then bade I him to go, sith what must be
None may prevent: and from my chamber door
He passed: and soon was armed: and forth went he,
Whom living on this earth I saw no more.

VII. — HOW MANO FOUND DIANTHA WITH THE PEASANTS IN THE WOOD: AND HIMSELF WAS TAKEN PRISONER BY THE LORDS.

OH, sweetest known of men, now must I tell
 How fate captived and put thee in her cart,
And at the wheel tolled her funereal bell:
 Oh thou, that wast the nearest to my heart,
My pitied one, my brave, my note of praise,
Who on that destined day from me didst part!
 This destined man fared forth upon the ways,
But met no living wight the silent day:
And but_whenas the night began to raise

Her black escutcheon over vesper grey,
Calling up blots that in the soft air spread,
And swept the sunlight gradually away:
Then entered he a forest dark and dread,
Of lonely passage and sad scenery,
By banks and dales where rushes grow to head:
Through little streams that bubbled secretly,
By thickening trees, which now the way denied,
For many hours with travel sore went he,
Nor sign of man in all the weald descried;
Yet held he on, as knowing well the while
That men were hidden in the covert wide.

And last he reached a place where in close file
The trees seemed wattled up with underwood:
And, slowly pushing through the rough-paled pile,
Straightway within a cleared space he stood;
And saw a fire, whose flame the trees displayed
Standing in circuit, an enclosing wood,
With openings in their boughs of darker shade:
Sad-eyed, annose, their giant arms they raised
O'er him who dared their secret haunt invade.

But there were other eyes that on him gazed,
And arms uplifted in more dangerous threat:
For in the clearing, round the fire that blazed,
The peasants in assembly wild were met:
The carlots who first raised that meteor vain
Which Robert caused in bloody mists to set:
They whom distress and poverty constrain
Against the seigneurs and their heavy dues
To meet in conjuration, and complain:
Whence war, defeat, ruin, and foul misuse
Of victory upon them overthrown;

Whom Robert, he of Rouen, did abuse.
Tortures and deaths he dealt before unknown
Even in this age of blood.and dismal deed:
Of which thing all the woe cannot be shown
To hurt the eyes of those who choose to read:
And though't was deemed quenched and in blood washed out,
The bitter cure did not at once succeed,
Nor the last vestige of the fever dout:
For still with secret arms, and hearts of fire,
The peasants met, the ways and woods about.
Whence this assembly, where with wild desire
They of their wants consult. What wonder then
That cries of tumult and ferocious ire
Broke forth amid those wild and desperate men,
Whenas the knight drew up with sudden rein
Within the precinct of their hidden den,
And sat back on his horse with musing mien?
Anon with knives uplifted two of them,
Backing each other, came on him amain,
In mind the rider or the horse to maim;
Lean varlets were they both, in ragged gear.
But he with drawn sword put away their aim,
Sparing to smite them, though they hung anear:
And cried aloud, "Oh, lamentable crew,
Consider well what thing in me ye fear;
"Think, if ye take my life, what deed ye do.
I am not of the number of your sieurs,
Whose rigour wrings revenge of yours from you.
"Nothing perforce hold I from you of yours.
No land have I to levy tax or toll.
But true it is that he the worst endures,
"Whose hostile semblance blots the mind's control,

And gives him hostile, all he friendly be :
And so these arms belie my pitying soul."
  Hereat they paused, and stood at gaze to see :
And then the peasant leader drew anear,
And gan demand what person he might be.
 But while he question made with look severe,
A woman came beside and curiously
Under the helmet of the knight gan peer :
 Then lightly laughed. "' 'Tis Mano," thus cried she,
" Thou, Elfeg, shalt not kill him for my sake :
Nor spy, nor traitor, nor hard lord is he,
 " But that most silly man, who me did take
From Italy, and brought me thitherward
With trouble sore, that I for him still make.
 " What, Mano, knowest thou not whom thou didst guard
So soberly, who ran from thee at last ?
Truly a tender charge hadst thou in ward,
 " Who might support nor heat nor chilly blast :
Though in these woods since then the bitter round
Of all the seasons four she hath o'erpassed."
  With that she bent her face toward the ground
A moment: then looked up with haughty head :
" Take him, and guard him well ; but never wound."
  Then, looking long on her, Sir Mano said,
" Diantha, if thou foundest me whilere
Neither unkind, nor by thy wiles misled,
 "Such find me now, when unto thee I swear
That now shall be performed what erst I swore,
The charge which from thy father yet I bear,
 " To bring thee back, and to thy place restore.
And thou, the more that thou hast evil done,
Wash out the same by reparation more."

When this she heard, much laughed that wicked one,
And circled off from him, and kept aloof:
But stedfast there he sat, and all did shun
    To put his arms of knighthood to the proof,
Armed but with knives and poles, and clad in skin.
Then from his stedfast look fearing reproof
    (As virtue ever hath the bet of sin)
She taketh by the hand her paramour,
Elfeg that hight, and to the knight did win;
    And much she urged, that she might 'scape that hour,
And live in wood with that strong caitiff lewd
To whom she pleased to give her beauty's dower.
    All which Sir Mano would not: yet he viewed
The while her beauty with full wonderment:
For never yet was seen in sted so rude
    So fair a creature, nor on earth yet sent.
Clad was she in grey dress, with bodden hood
Of crimson, as his dream did her present.
    Full grown was she to the wide open bud
Which beauty in her summer bears to sight:
Red were her cheeks in newest womanhood:
    Her eyes were like two stars of piercing light:
Which now she strove to soften in appeal
Unto the mercy of the grave-browed knight.
    But he with whom she stood was one to steel
All pity in a mind that could descry
The inward treasure through the outer seal.
    He was not young, compared with her, pardy:
Nor yet with Mano: but nigh thirty years:
His hair was reddish, rusty, tossed on high;
    And round his eyes were scattered loathly hairs,
Both brow and lashes: which stood thick and long;

Like to the beetle, when in rage he rears.
To his red eyeballs did of right belong
Down-glancing cunning and fierce villany.
Rough was his shape : his joints were big and strong :
And in clay-coloured camise clad was he.
  Such varlet this high maiden chose for mate,
I know not by what spell of mastery.
Neither may I conjecture nor relate
What had the sequel of that business been,
If it had lain with Mano to debate.
  For other thing fell out. With dagger keen
The varlet ran from her whose hand he held,
And stabbed the knight's horse, where, the reins between,
  His proud neck o'er his mighty muscles swelled.
Up to the haft he plunged and left the knife,
Then ran aside : no skill such blow withheld.
  Upreared the destrier proud in bloody strife,
With rolling eyeballs a wild moment's space,
Then, falling on the steel, struck out his life.
  And Mano was cast down upon his face :
Yet even as rose the horse, flatling his stroke
Caught that false varlet in his middle race :
  And with some force falling his wrist it broke.
  Then Mano quickly rose : and was in doubt
Whether with sword that felon to avoke,
  Ere the wild people closed himself about,
Or seize the maiden, and make thence his way.
But at that beat of time a dismal rout
  Began upon the part from him away ;
And there he saw a throng of knights in field,
Who in mid charge did cast down all and slay :
  Slew all, and mercy unto none would yield.

These were the lords, who had approached unknown
The assembly of the peasants in the weald.
   Them Robert sent, to whom the place was shown
By traitorous tongue, or his own industry :
And his fell mind was planted in each one.
   Sworn to spare none that living there might be,
They slew the most that were upon the ground,
And all the rest they hanged upon tree :
   Then beat with dogs the woods that were around,
So that there thence escaped scarce two or three.
Which when he saw begun, Mano best found
   To snatch Diantha up, and thence to flee.
      But little space had he accomplished,
As through the wood his burdened way made he;
   When of a knight he was encountered,
Who lay in wait for those who fled thereby.
Then battle rose, and heavy strokes were sped :
   Which to the opposer ended fatally :
For Mano by main force beat down the man,
And slew him there : a deadly victory:
   That man alone was slain of those that wan
The field against the peasants poor and bare :
He only against iron armour ran.
      But when that driving fight first dinned the air,
Diantha from the knight away was slid,
And toward the open weald did back repair,
   Seeking where yet her losel love were hid.
Whom as Sir Mano missed, thither he hied,
Resolved that she of him should not be rid.
   And as he searched the place from side to side,
There, to make short of long, was he waylaid
By many knights at once who him espied.

So destiny devised: at him they made,
And rode him down upon the open plain:
That in his harness sorely crushed and brayed
Captived was he, and bound with heavy chain.

VIII.—HOW DIANTHA FARED IN CAPTIVITY: AND HOW MANO.

OF all that living in that wood met late,
That conclave wild, were left but two alone,
Mano, with whom Diantha, caught by fate.
 The rest from life by various deaths were gone:
The most with deadly swathes the field did deck,
Part in the underwood made their last moan,
 Part on the trees were hanging by the neck
(The dearnliest sight of all were they to see,)
And this great cruelty no man did check.
 Sir Mano, lying bound upon the lea,
Expected his own stroke to come anon:
For drunken seemed those lords with cruelty;
 And rode about, smiting where life was none.
But presently he was conveyed from thence,
And carried to a dungeon of thick stone,
 Within a lord's near dwelling of defence:
Where too Diantha, in that house of pain,
Not far from him kept forced residence.
 She changed for prison strait the open plain,
Lamenting Elfeg, whom a furious knight
Upon the battlefield outright had slain:
 And hating Mano with redoubled spite,
As cause of these new woes that her oppressed.
   Nor long before the lords a message write
To Robert of Rouen, and his will request

Touching their captives. He in brief replies
That death by burning was for both his hest:
 For him, as fautor of conspiracies,
And slayer of a knight full well renowned,
And taking part against high dignities:
 For her, because she was the leman found
Of the ringleader of their enemies,
And from high birth had grovelled low to ground
 (A sin above all sins to noble eyes).
Wherefore for both of them this cruel death
By next convenient hour doth he advise.
       Which when Diantha heard, she veiled uneath
Her eyes from laughter at the fell intent,
Well knowing that while love in man did breathe,
 So fair a form as hers should not be shent.
For she already with the castellan
Was plotting freedom from imprisonment:
 And her looks fired with love that fiery man,
A lord unused to have his pleasure fail:
But what they planned, and how fell out their plan,
 Shall in the sequel due be told in tale.—
Compared with beauty, in the hour of need
What merchandise has worth that may avail?
       When Mano heard the doom that was decreed,
He also smiled, as if his inmost heart
Took some resolve of counsel and good heed,
 Nor from himself through false fear would depart,
Albeit death so horrible might fear
A mind that never would in battle start.
 Leave asked he then to write from dungeon drear
A letter to the man who did him dead:
And in the same he had a purpose clear,

Against himself all evils that were laid
First to admit, and more to add indeed
Than were in Robert's heavy sentence read :
How with the peasants he in heart agreed
Against the lords in undertakings all :
How on the lords great vengeance was decreed :
　That this last slaughter, which in the wood did fall,
Was but a foul deed done : that justice great
He for himself required, with fair trial.
　　　　For 'twas his drift in this to exaggerate
Upon himself both guilt and innocence,
That he Diantha might redeem from fate
　By drawing on himself all violence.
Of her he added these : That howsoe'er
It stood with him, in her was none offence,
　Who was a maiden noble, rich, and fair,
The daughter of a lord in honour high,
Though she were gathered in some demon's snare,
　And fell away from her high dignity :
And he demanded, as of right, therefor,
That upon her were done no felony,
　But to her father they should her restore.
—Thus wrote he, weening in this way to bring
Diantha back to safety and honour.
　　　　But when in Rouen Robert read this thing,
He sent his Fool to answer it ; who came
Riding upon an ass, with reins of string,
　Attired in a gown of painted flame,
Wearing at heel a silly wooden prong
In lieu of knightly spur : a form of shame.
　Small, and deformed was he, yet lithe and strong,
And in his face was malice infinite :

And as he rode, he sounded on a gong;
And bore a bladder halbert, as a knight.
This shameful creature rode up to the gate,
Leaving his wayward steed, there to alight.
  He entered into Mano's prison straight,
Crying, " Ho, Mano, father sends thee me
For answer; other answer thou mayst wait:
  "And yet right well shalt thou purveyed be."
To call Count Robert father, to his brain
Seemed good to be repeated endlessly.
Now leave we here Sir Mano with this bane.

IX.—HOW JOANNA FARED IN THE CONVENT: AND
  HOW SHE DISCOVERED MANO'S PARENTAGE.

AND turn we to Joanna, left behind
  This long while in my writing, from the day
That she to Gerbert dared the love unbind,
  Which she for Mano cherishing let prey
Upon her tender heart right wretchedly:
And then had been by Gerbert swept away
  Into a secret place of nunnery,
Which hight Beyond Four Rivers: there she stayed,
Pining her tender heart in malady.
  Thus Gerbert's first intention was delayed,
To cure her love: could love desert his throne
While expectation still his realm upstayed?
  For of the knight though tidings heard she none,
Yet knew she not that Gerbert ne'er had ta'en
Any meet cause or fit occasion
  Her trembling heart to Mano to make plain,
The which she hoped, what time she made it known,

And let her sick mind to his ear complain.
Though all was covered now like buried stone,
Yet oft she looked upon that sealèd scroll
Which holy Gerbert gave to her alone,
And at the time forbade her to unroll
Ere either from himself commandment came,
Or that she heard of his death-parted soul.
Full oft her sad eyes rested on the same,
And her hands handled it, and pressed it close
Upon her bosom and heart's aching flame.
        But when no rede she heard, nor yet arose
The sun that set on Gerbert's wondrous doom,
This lingering hope within her slowly froze.
  Then paleness gan her gentle youth consume,
And that small scroll was torment, sith she knew
That all that she should know therein had room.
  Oh limit of strict fate! was it then heaven's due,
Gerbert, to hold that faithful love concealed,
Which maiden heart trembled to thee to show?
  To bid her hold a secret ever sealed,
Which all too late to knowledge came at last,
As that may poison worst that best had healed?
      For now, when Mano was in prison fast,
Sentenced to death, and waiting for his end,
Throughout all lands the wondrous rumour passed
  How Gerbert from the earth with fiends did wend:
Which awful thing, by all men now averred,
I neither here affirm, nor yet defend:
  But this I say, that no man better heard
Than Gerbert of those friends who knew him well,
Albeit that he in Mano greatly erred.
  And here most part, methinks, 'twas Fortune's spell

Which him who elsewhere ever nobly dealt,
Evilly to deal in this man did compel.
Full often policy her sway hath felt
To single men destructive and severe;
And public care Love's waxen wings may melt.
  But when Joanna heard this rumour clear,
With shaking hand the secret gan she feel,
If still it lay upon her breast of fear.
  A moment, and she doth the wax unseal,
And read the writing of the more than dead,
While joy and wonder through her bosom steal.
  For to this end was written what she read:
That Mano was of the old Duke Richard son
By one whom he by guile, not ring, had wed,
  Hight Harleve: who did henceforth all men shun,
And thence set forth in foreign lands to fare,
Where double fruit from her beheld the sun,
  A boy and girl, whom she expired to bear:
That thus much to the old Duke had been known,
Namely, the birth of them, the death of her:
  Who, in his penitence, the same had shown
To Gerbert, bidding him the children seek,
That he through them the mother might atone:
  That of the girl no tidings were to speak:
But that the boy in low estate was found,
And long time tossed in Fortune's tempest bleak,
  Now grown a knight, noble as stood on ground,
Namely, that Mano who in Italy
With Thurold kept the Norman marches round:
  That therefore to the young Duke Richard he
Half-brother was, and to the Archbishop,
Robert of Rouen, in the same degree:

Commending him to them, the scroll did stop :
And it was signed with Gerbert's hand and ring,
And to those twain *Salutem* gave atop.
   Another writing was there, carrying
Unto Joanna further solacement :
That hitherto Gerbert had kept this thing
 Hidden from all, through politic intent
That Mano might with single mind fulfil
Those ends for which his life was to be spent ;
 And of the sacred vow be mindful still
Whereby he mindful was to dedicate
Who reared him, and for precept did instil
 To be of Holy Church a champion great :—
But that henceforth his own will might he use
(Being hence absolved from service high and strait);
 What earthly lot he would to take and choose :
And, if he chose that maid who loved him well,
His master there to smile would not refuse.
   Which when Joanna read, adown she fell
In a great swoon for joy and fluttered heart :
But rose anon more quicklier than I tell :
 And from that house made ready to depart :
To seek the Archbishop and the Duke : and so
To Rouen was she bound, as to the mart
Where she for happiness should barter woe.

X.—CONCERNING JOANNA IN THE NUNNERY.

DARK-WORKING Fate, who turnest with thy hand
 The spherèd stars that measure human days,
How may we know thy work, or understand
 (As He who set thee on the cosmic ways)

The lot that thou dost portion out to each,
The lines that thou dost spin in thy dark maze?
  Day tells to day of heaven the voice and speech,
Alas! we see the star, but not the sphere,
Nor thy dark hand, which toward it thou dost reach:
  Only those shining points to us appear
Which therefore we deem all: but still unkenned
The subtler fatal ether doth career.
            That which befell Joanna must be penned,
Which showed thy dark contrary influence,
While she in convent her sad days did spend.
  Long ere that day that she departed thence
Came those which doubled all her grief of mind,
And made more wretched her sad residence.
            There was a priest who oft would entrance find
Into that house reputed most severe,
Who being to evil in his thoughts inclined,
  As by his office given to holy prayer,
Some harm occasioned in that place, 'twas said,
With some who like himself in nature were—
  Which were it so or not, his siege he laid
Against Joanna, when she thither came,
Leaving all else for love of that sweet maid.
  With thought of her he did his mind inflame;
And presently to urge her gan presume,
Bold from his former use, with words of blame:
  Bidding her in her mind for love make room,
Nor leave his solace to a day too late,
Nor still in solitude her youth consume:
  Lest dreariness should penitence create,
And peace deceptive fly from her anon,
While weary years drew on to listless date.

Then quickly bade she that ill man begone:
Who, smiling, took his way: yet would renew
His former talk upon occasion.
And when unto a sister there she flew,
No comfort got she, nor direction clear
To make to cease from her this misery new.
And more I cannot tell: suffice it here
That from that hour the sad Joanna hid
This trouble in her breast: nor would appear,
Nor quit her cell, but if some duty bid;
Nor ever on that man would cast her eyes,
Nor walk with any there that companied.
Which when the man perceived, and with surprise
Found her pure soul locked up in deep offence,
Rage, hatred, filled him: now would he despise
That which with black care truly charged his sense.
But when despite could not with care contend
Then rage put off despiteous pretence,
And hatred stood confirmed: he gan to spend
Long days devising how himself to wreak
Upon that creature mild: but, to make end,
Nor further in his wretched mind to seek,
His purposed hate was turned to love again,
Whenas he saw her face, or heard her speak.
If he heard others wroth with her disdain,
Or whatso chance it were, I little trow
Which might his hate to love again constrain:
But thenceforth love, who oft the vile doth throw,
By the sight of lovely virtue, to despair,
Unto the point of madness urged his woe.
Thin grew he; wild his haggard eyes did glare,
And up and down he wandered nights and days,

Seeking some glimpse of her who was his care.
Insomuch that his altered looks and ways
To those who hitherto found better cheer
In him, wrought wonder, and mislike gan raise.
  Thus went the time : and the disease more near
On his dark mind, like ravening thing, did cling.
To chapel hied he nor for mass nor prayer,
 And of his functions would he not a thing :
Nor yet, again, would he his sickness own
Unto his piteous fellow's questioning.
 For now he feared to be shut up alone,
And lose those haggard walks, whereby each day
The harvest of new grief for him was sown.
  At length he heard Joanna gone away,
And never to return, what time the sound
Of Gerbert's end the hearts of all did fray.
 Which heard, since thus his last hope fell to ground,
He took to bed, complaining sickness sore ;
Where by his fellow he was warmly wound,
 And with exceeding love nursed evermore,
Fed with soft meats, and watched,—his fellow there,
Who by his brother chaplain set great store.
 And well indeed the other seemed to fare,
Eating whatever to his mouth was brought :
But not the lighter grew his keeper's care :
 For nought the weakness lessened : and him thought
That in his face such wanness should not be,
And marvelled how the sickness with him wrought.
  Till once, returning from the chapelry
Into the chamber where the sick man lay,
A darksome streak like blood he chanced to see,
 Which from beneath the bed was making way.

Whereat the man a knife unto him showed,
And to him said, "Brother, I did but play
  With thy great love, which has to me o'erflowed:
For other love hath shent me: I am slain
For love which I to cherish never owed.
  "Her love I, who went hence, nor comes again;
Whom I essayed, and being but denied,
Great malice showed her, which I rue in vain.
  " For her I slay myself, well satisfied :
The poor requital of my parting breath
I give for lust, malice, and evil pride."
    And from what else the man said in his death,
It seemed that he this knife in secret caught,
And every day the coverlet beneath
  A wound therewith upon his body wrought:
So by degrees his life all flowed away,
And he into extremity was brought.
    This grisly thing made noise enow that day,
Seeming to be of utter cruelty,
That one should dare himself thus cut and slay.
God's hand keep all men from God's enemy.

XI.—HOW JOANNA WENT TO ROUEN TO SAVE SIR
    MANO, AND HOW SHE SPED.

MEANWHILE the glad Joanna took her road
    Toward Rouen, bearing forth that writing rare
Which held Sir Mano's story, and him showed
  Both with the Archbishop and the Duke to share
A father's heart, a brother's part to claim.
To give this to Duke Richard was her care,
  Or to Lord Robert, when she thither came :
But best she hoped the Duke in place to find,

Who might with gentler grace receive the same:
(For Richard ever gentle was and kind,)
But he was absent on a hunting great,
So fell it not according to her mind.
   And on that prelate proud alone to wait,
Destiny hastened her, and she full soon
By right of beauty passed his palace gate.
      That cruel man, receiving her anon
With gentleness (such power had beauty tho')
Her tidings read: then in his grey eyes shone
   A laughing spark of doubt: and round did go
Those puckering wrinkles which sprang instantly,
If aught misliked him, and sped to and fro.
   Doubt only grew in him from testimony,
The while she heard with horrible dismay
From his hard lips, swollen and stiff to see,
   How under deadly sentence Mano lay:
His insurrection with the peasants made,
The slaying of that knight he slew that day.
      But at this telling, though so sick dismayed,
That hardly she her shaking breast controlled,
Yet in brave speech she strove, and sternly bade
   The man to save his brother true and bold,
And give him welcome to his high estate,
As he his father's name in love would hold.
   She bade him his mild brother imitate,
(His brother eke) most gentle and sincere,
As he his own renown on high did rate:
   She said that he was God's high overseer:
And all she added else that best might weigh
With one who kept for honour open ear.
      He, marking her more than what she might say,

Yet answered her with promise good and fair,
And bade her come again at no long day :
He said that he his purpose would declare
In that behalf whereof she made request,
And in the meantime bade her have less care.
 So went the dove from out the vulture's nest,
Resolved with earliest light to come again,
And find in what design he seemed to rest.
  With earliest light she came again, certain,
And was received with more joyful cheer
Than her the former day did entertain.
 He said that Mano's lineage stood clear
In his belief : that messengers were gone
To set him free withouten let or fear :
 And that he might those rights assume anon
Which should to him out of all doubt belong,
As he to princes brother was and son.
  Which lying guile wrought joy so high and strong
In poor Joanna, that her eyes gan glow
With radiance that had been away too long :
 Her cheeks in colour rose, long pined with woe,
So that he thought was never aught so fair :
And bade her not with hurry thence to go.
 But never could she stay, secure of care,
Whilst all in issue hung : eager of heart
Thither, where lay Sir Mano to repair.,
 So from the palace gate she doth depart
Though hardly granted thence : but her intent
To go to Mano doth no thing impart.
  So she her way to Mano's prison went
Leaving the bishop and his guileful mind,
Who one true thing in all ne said ne meant.

For whether he to evil were inclined
For love of it, and cruelty preferred
Of malice, and an instinct brute and blind;
　Or whether that old hate within him stirred,
Which he to Thurold owed in former days:
Or whether he misdoubted Gerbert's word,
　(Gerbert, whom he misliked in sundry ways)
Concerning Mano and his parentage,
Nor would from him accept Sir Mano's praise:
　Uncertain is, nor need a thought engage.
But to stay Mano's death, or set him free
'Tis certain that he sent no embassage.
　'Twere poor to ask what wrought with such as he,
Yet, might I judge, he acted in this wise
Mostly from simple incredulity,
　Not out of hate: because that in his eyes
What Gerbert wrote appeared incredible.
For cold the heart that steeped in pleasure lies,
　And unbelief and doubt the closest dwell
Within the baser mind and duller head.
These are Fate's hammers: accident her bell.—
　　Fate beat her bell, the death of her doomed dead.
If Robert had been forth, Richard at home,
And each had acted in the other's stead,
　Then truly had another end been come
To sad Joanna's quest: Richard's true eyes
Had seen the truth, and stayed the impending doom.
　　Fair was Joanna ever, I avise:
But I have heard of certain that e'en now
Her day of fairest beauty seemed to rise,
　When sorrow and long love had made her brow
Tenderly radiant, as the hanging skies

When the south wind moves every wingèd bough :
Such o'er the changing wood the May cloud flies,
Soft, bright, and light, was she : one lovely fold,
That seemed to gather to grave thought her eyes,
Of bygone sorrow and old anguish told,
One sweet contraction, delicate and fine :
But youth to bear love's burden still is bold :—
Her looks were strong ('tis age that has to pine)
Her eyes were quick, and lightsome as of yore,
Her rounded cheeks as perfect in their line :
Her step was like the deer on ferny floor,
Her figure tall, and like a balanced tower,
Which from his place seems stepping evermore,
So wondrously 'tis fashioned through art's power.—
She had those years which bring to perfectness :
And stood full blown, like to the lily's flower.
Ah ! now consider well in her fair dress
This lily of earth's field, her lovely head
Who rears amid the waste, companionless :
Wide open stands her heart : no secret dread
Bids her enfold her petals, like the rose,
Over her golden bosom undismayed.
Oh, undefended thus to friends or foes,
Shall she endure, then, in her perfect state,
Until she ripen to a timely close,
By the kind season carried to her date ;
Or must she tremble on her lofty stem
At the rough hand of sudden-working Fate,
Scattering to the winds her diadem,
Brushing the tender gold-bloom from her heart ;
And die in her full hour, a perfect gem,
In whose fair essence all sweet things have part ?

XII.—HOW JOANNA WENT TO MANO.

WHEN in the wailful winds of autumn tide
   This maiden sought her love in jeopardy,
What thing then met she in her hasty ride
   Bodeful of evil and calamity?
Sith never yet came evil without sign,
If to the eye be given that to see,
   Though love and hope but little can divine.
— Upon a thorn a corby black of blee
She saw, who turned about his curious eyne:
   Full big he sat upon the little tree,
Balancing in the wind his heavy form:
But, on her coming, flew off heavily.
   — Far flew he down the thickness of the storm,
And she his look no more in memory held,
But most of her long voyage did perform:
   When, lo, another thing that she beheld!
Which was a stake new planted in the ground,
Or else a tree whose boughs the axe had felled:
   On whose smooth top that bird a perch had found,
Which to maintain his mighty wings he waved,
Till she drew nigh, when them to flight he wound,
   Losing by wings what he by wings had saved.
Then wonder rose in her, and shaking doubt,
While down the wind slow went the bird depraved.
         Now she beholds the castle square and stout
Wherein Sir Mano lay—her journey's end;
And still that fowl afar the air did flout:
   But when she took it in her eyelids' bend,
He vanished from her sight with darkest note:

And the strong castle gan his mass protend.
  High were the walls in view, and broad the moat,
And many towers on either flank she sees
Whose flags upon the tossed sky wave and float.
  The leaden roofs arose like terraces
Behind the battlements; and many knights
Were moving in those airy galleries.
  And when she came more close beneath their heights,
With warning of her coming even then
The trumpet sounded in the armed sites.
  But the awakened tumult ceased again,
As through the crowded gate anon she passed,
And lodge, which swarmed with idle laughing men.
      She entered thus into the courtyard vast,
And for the captive Mano did require,
Whom soon she found in lonely dungeon cast,
  (The way being opened at her fierce desire,)
And on her knees she flung herself beside
The enchained knight, with heart and eyes of fire;
  Being all amazed, but not yet terrified
To see him in such case. "Mano," she said,
" Why dost thou yet in prison's dark abide?
  "Hath then the messenger so idly sped,
Bearing thy pardon and thy life to thee,
To raise thee from this floor to honour's head?
  "Then first am I (as fitteth in love's gre)
To tell thee of the dawning happy day
That lifts thee up."—"Joanna," answered he,
  "Nothing know I of that thou seemest to say:
But now, thy face to see, thy hand to press,
Drives questioning with misery away:
  "And all my heart is filled with happiness.

N

For so I love thee that I seem ere now
Not to have loved before."—" Nevertheless,"
　So answered she with tears, " answer me thou
That which I ask, ere I that love shall tell
Which holds me wholly, and to thee avow :
" For dreadful fear in me begins to dwell,
Seeing thee thus, who thought to find thee free."
—" I only know that from this darksome cell,"
　He answered, "doom to-morrow carries me :
And sad it seemed, before thy lovely face
Made darkness light, and prison liberty ! "
　　Then she in agony began to trace
Of Gerbert's actions all the history,
Since she at first in Rouen sought his grace :—
　How she before him laid her misery,
In hope that he to Mano would declare
And make it known : (" No whit of this," quoth he,
　" Ere this dear moment ever reached mine ear.")
How then he sent her into nunnery,
Where long the time she lingered in despair
　Till his own death ; what thence there came to be,—
The unsealed writing, the Archbishop's share,
Her journey hither made in secrecy,
　To find him free from peril and from care.—
All this with gasps, and twisted hands she told :
Such pain such tender bosom ill might bear.
　　　Then Mano said, " For what thou dost unfold,
Oh more than sister, loved and honoured more,
Concerning Gerbert, I my speech withhold ;
　" (For he is dead, and was my friend of yore).
But little hope I from my brother new ;
He has deceived thee, or this prison door

"Would never hold me now if he were true.
Therefore in thy sweet converse let me live
Tenfold the hours that still to life are due."
 Hereat Joanna a great cry did give,
And sprang from him: in haste was she to go
And from the castellan demand reprieve,
 Ere the next morning brought the instant blow.
But Mano stayed her: "Sweet Joanna, stay.
Hear yet the sequel which I shall bestow:
 "Diantha, Thurold's child, shares my sad day,
Caught in the pagan weald along with me:
She who from Richard's court did whilom stray.
 "Her have I yet in charge to Italy
To render back: whereto an oath I sware,
And, seeking her, fell in this jeopardy.
 "If therefore thou canst aught, be it for her:
Set her in freedom, let her home retire.
But if thou canst no way to safety steer,
 "Because the fire is bitter (yea, the fire,
As I must say, for both of us decreed)
Give her this poisoned ring at my desire,
 "Which well shall serve her at the utmost need.
I had it from a man, a forester,
Found dying in the woods from savage deed.
 "He gave it: whom being dead did I inter.
Virtuous it is to end the life at once
Without one pain, he being the answerer."
 Thereto Joanna uttered no response:
But flung herself from him, and thence she went:
And to the courtyard of the castle runs,
 As frantic by the danger imminent.

XIII. — CONCERNING DIANTHA, HOW SHE ESCAPED, AND TO WHAT END SHE CAME.

GRIM Fate henceforth her quarry gan to ply
 In sterner sort; more earnest looking now,
Her prey she faced, whitherso it would fly :
 Her eye that had but glanced began to glow :
And now her ending stroke did she prepare,
After her play, which wrought but wounds and woe.
 Meanwhile Diantha in the prison where
She lay immured, expected the same end:
And yet in truth she felt but little care :
 For by her beauty she had gained for friend
The ruler of the castle, that young lord,
Who mad with love vowed death from her to fend.
 He now was come, obedient to his word,
To lead her forth from dreadful death to light,
What time Joanna wildly sped abroad.
 In secret came he in the midst of night,
And passed by stealth toward her high-towered cell
By countless steps that reached the castle's height.
 He found her soft hand in the stony well,
Drew sweetly her long arm through his own hand,
Till round her yielded form his strong arm fell.
 Thus on the topmost turret stairs they stand ;
Then down they steal in hush of silence deep.
Alas! in vain their care: an armed band
 Awaited them below the stairway steep,
When at the bottom they arrived were,
And in the dusk abroad began to peep.
 Then an old knight full stern his hand did rear

Against this lord's breast, whispering, " Madness great
Is on thee, sure, Eustace, my nephew dear.
" How many scores of knights within thy gate
Upon this grave occasion are met,
And this exemplar punishment await?
" If of to-morrow's promise they be let,
If traitor to thy order thee they find,
How will they rage, what vengeance will they whet!
" But fear not that : for here with faithful mind
Thy kinsmen only stand : none other, lo !
If but this folly be betimes resigned."
  Thus said he : and the other did forego
His promised prize, with bitter raging pain :
No other might be : many stood below.
  So was Diantha back to prison ta'en.—
Who then their meditated flight betrayed?
The Fool of Robert 'twas that wrought their bane.
 For he, who for the most part wait had laid
By Mano's door, keeping malignant watch,
And with shrill yells and laughter his ears brayed,
 Nevertheless some moments found to snatch
To jeer Diantha with his wondrous tongue ;
And thus her plot of flight in mind gan catch.
 He saw Sir Eustace, that castellan young,
Nigh hand : and carried this to that old knight,
His uncle stern, to whom the song he sung.
  That was the time, before the fall of night,
When he was busy in his meddling spleen,
That poor Joanna came to Mano's sight,
 Nor was by that malicious antic seen :
And when she left the imprisoned knight again,
He went back thither with his gibings keen.

So chanced it that she never came in ken.
But she went forth into the sanded yard,
And heard the angry voices of those men:
And after found Sir Eustace panting hard,
And raging idly with his lossful gain:
Him in the dark her eyes with care regard.—
She knew him for the gentle lord, certain,
Who had not letted her from Mano's cell;
And hope rose in her, aid from him to gain.
Therefore her voice, softer than silver bell,
Stole to his ear, while she for pity pled,
Almost invisible, scarce audible.
The sore man thereupon being comforted,
She promised him that he his love should win
If only to her counsel he obeyed:
To which he well agreed : then, to begin,
Her in Diantha's cell she bade him place:—
And he led her up the stair the tower within.
A soldier there, whose feet they heard to pace,
Refused her not, nor would her passage stay,
For him she won by largess and mere grace,
Saying, that nought she meant him to betray,
Nor cause him scath, if but for moments few
With the condemned maid she might delay.
—But ere she went, her step she yet withdrew
Unto Sir Eustace, and into his hand
Laid Mano's ring, saying, " As thou art true
" I charge thee ; yea, as thou to God shalt stand,
Bear this to Mano: bid him use it so
As he to other's use did it remand."
       Then up the narrower stairway did she go,
Leaving him there to wait her quick return:

Nor long he waited in his place below,
  Where the steep windings left a shady turn,
When forth she issued on the downward way,
  And in his hand he felt her touch to burn.
Full well he seemed to know, the truth to say,
That tender yielding hand, the which he pressed :
Yes, 'twas Diantha's hand in his that lay.
  Then gasping joy rose in him, when he guessed :
But horror soon and pity swelled his tide
For her by whose undoing he was blessed.
  But in that place not long might they abide :
He led, and set her on Joanna's beast;
  And to the gate in courtesy did guide ;
  And saw her soon into the world released ;
The warders knowing nought of all the thing,
And seeing but their master speed his guest.
  And, to make short this story's wandering,
In foreign lands Sir Eustace went to her
After the day that Mano's death did bring.
  He went to her, and was the messenger
Of Mano's and Joanna's tragedy;
But he had lost the love that was whilere,
  For he was changed by all that misery,
And to have married her, or otherwise
Enjoyed her love, he deemed mere infamy.
  And he so wrought with her, that she likewise
Was changed in heart, and all her follies old
With scorpion whip her conscience did chastise.
  Wherefore their course most chastely they did hold
To Italy : where she her father met,
Whom she had left so long, the Count Thurold.
  And thus Sir Mano did discharge his debt,

If not in person, yet by deputy,
Her in her father's house again to set.
   And not long thence Count Thurold fell to die,
And in her arms he died : and she thereon
To convent went, and lived in sanctity,
   Till eke by her the better world was won.
And Eustace, he became a hermit great,
Of blessed memory for alms deeds done:
   Unto the poor he parted his estate,
Lived in the wild, and was of people sought
For his wise redes and heart compassionate.
And thus with these it ended as it ought.

XIV.—CONCERNING MANO IN PRISON.

FELICITY, best gift of God to man,
   Perfectest creature, who in thy fair form
Holdest so many with harmonious plan,
   And art a well-trimmed ship to ride the storm,
Bear thou the things which seem to do thee wrong,
When Virtue's ark woe's deluges deform.
   Oh, bear a while with me in this sad song,
Which shows thee of less might than crooked Fate :
For out of weakness still thou waxest strong.
             Now is Diantha through the castle gate
Passed as Joanna, and to safety fled ;
And Eustace left amazed in dolour great.
   He to Sir Mano's prison quickly sped,
The ring to give, and what he knew to say,
Which little aided his forecasting head,
   Not knowing who might be that stranger may,

Who took on her such dreadful penalty;
But now no further knowledge get he may:
 For there the fool of Robert doth he see,
Who kept his post, nor from it budged a whit,[1]
But welcomed him with hideous mockery,
 Feigning indeed that he was come for it,
That he with him the captive might deride:
Whom Eustace neither to drive out thought fit,
 Lest his loud cries should raise the hostile side,
Nor might before him any question make:
Therefore in ignorance he must abide.
 The ring he gave: the which did Mano take,
Much marvelling to see it come again:
For, first, he deemed Joanna, for his sake,
 Might not perform as she had underta'en,
So was departed, leaving him alone:
Nor knew he whom he saw, what man of men.
 For Eustace stood like a dark-written stone,
Spake not, but looked with sorrow bursting out:
So that Joanna gone, Joanna gone,
 Grew sorrowfully sure his heart about.
Also he thought again, the case might be
Diantha chose to die that aid without;
 He thought his own gift sent back scornfully,
And much it grieved him that she should refuse
All that he could in their extremity.
  But he resolved never the same to use,
For since a tender may to bear the fire,
Contemning poison's succour, dared to choose,
 Like courage should a manly breast inspire:
" Yea, I will suffer all the worst that man
Hath ever borne, since so doth Fate require:

"And it occasion grant" (occasion can,—
So in his mind he argues) "when at stake
We burn together"——he to shortest span
Would bring her pains, and with that potion slake:
And her vowed safety to his power complete.
Thus thinking he in hand the ring doth take.
    Then went Sir Eustace with unwilling feet,
And left him in the dungeon to his doom,
Whenas the morning on those bars gan beat,
  Cloud bars that hold the curtains of thin gloom—
And the pale early light broke overhead
Across the window of his narrow room.
    And long time after Mano had been dead,
With iron scratched upon the stony wall
Where he had been captived, these words were read:
  "I, who to Destiny was ever thrall,
End by her deed my course by her begun:
And honours and desire of life let fall.

  "My day, which scarcely smiled at dawn, now run
To his long West, I see the night full near,
Which shall devour the brightness of my sun.
  "Now must I think that Death has strewn my bier:
Now must I part from glory that I won:
And miss achievement that I held most dear.
  "Glory with shame, as life with death, foredone,
Bids me make haste, and hasteneth my way:
I go the limit whither these are gone.
  "Now youth his age doth meet before his day:
My faith so true doth faith to me deny:
Love flies me now, that never was at stay,
And adds his vote that it is time to die."

XV.—THE DEATH OF MANO AND JOANNA.

THAT night of Spring, which had lain mildly down,
  Brought forth a morn of cold and bitter cheer :
For on the bed of Dawn gan Boreas frown,
  And pelted her with many a bolt severe,
Slinging his slanted sleet to scare away
Mild Zephyrus, that had been haunting near,
  Mild Zephyrus, bringer of softer day :
He on his watery-coloured pinions flew,
And into other regions took his way.
        Such was the day, born out of season due,
When Mano to his like and timeless end
Was hurled forth out of his iron mew.
  (Ah, woefulness which only death may mend
Bids death make haste more deadliness to stay,
And struggling life from her poor haunt to send).
  He was brought forth at dawning of the day :
(Now sorrow fills me with her waymenting,
And bids me stint the things that I should say :
  He was my friend when life began to spring,
My comforter in peril, brave and sweet,
My company in weary wandering).
  Led on a cart he was, bound hands and feet,
And from the castle drawn unto the stake,
Guarded by knights on horses strong and fleet.
  A hundred round that sorry hearse did strake,
To execute on him their vengeance drear,
Who (as they deemed) did out of knighthood break.
  There Eustace rode, a wretched cavalier,
Surrounded by his kinsmen dour and stern :

And there the Fool, in his outlandish gear;
Whose folly ceaseless as his rage did burn.
A rebeck held he, and thereon he played,
Whilst still his glare on Mano would he turn.
He bitter jests and filthy scoffing made :
His ass, that felt full oft his kicking heel,
Amid the mighty horses ran and brayed.
Of Mano it was said that stone nor steel
No firmer countenance than he could show :
Nor he from silence did his lips unseal :
Save that to himself he smiled and muttered low,
"I feel the smell of nettles in warm shade."
This did I hear of him, and nothing mo.
And, thus unto the stake their voyage made,
There was he bound, and waiting death he stood :
And none might say they saw him aught dismayed.
 Anon, as he had seen her in the wood,
He seemed to see, approaching the same way,
Diantha, covered with her scarlet hood,
 And closely folded in her garments grey.
Who, being come, unto the stake was tied,
While all men made a space, and moved away.
And now the fire was to the pile applied :
Then, when it gan to blaze, and mounted high,
The scarlet hood fell from her face aside :
 And lo, Joanna ! It is said a cry
Came from Sir Mano; and with mighty strain
He burst the bands the which his hands did tie.
 Then to himself he drew her by the chain
Until her mouth kissed his : then suddenly
Into her mouth his fingers pressed amain :
 And she hung dead before the flame came nigh.

Then the flame reached: and he, standing upright,
Held down his hands, and suffered silently.
    This the last stroke of destiny's fell might
To die and slay his own dear love, would seem;
And like a felon, who was truest knight.
    But yet her death his promise did redeem
To bear Diantha to her father old :
And that much solace ye thereof may deem.
    And his conclusion happiness did hold,
To meet at last in death with blessed love,
And faith approved by death in death to fold.
    He saved from pain that tender-footed dove,
Not the wild bird of wilfulness and strife :
He died with pain, but raised all pain above,
And ending at the summit of man's life.

XVI. — HOW A FALSE TALE OF THEIR DEATH WAS TOLD, AND THEN THE TRUE: AND HOW THEY WERE BURIED.

THE sudden snow, which that one day appeared,
    By Boreas blown into the temperate Spring,
Ere from earth's mould it vanished and was cleared,
    For miles was strown by sparks and gledes burning
Shot down the wind : far o'er the crudded white
Cinder and sooty ash span blackening;
    And streams of dust and smoke, careering light
Reached even to the wood below the hill,
What time Duke Richard came thereof in sight.
    Then startling horror did Duke Richard fill,
And harder galloped he the wood beside,
The while his piercing spurs his courser thrill,

Foremost was he of all who there did ride,
Who came with him to stay that deadly doom :
Alas, too late, as Fortune bade betide !
   For he, whenas to Rouen he came home,
Was met by Robert with that history
Of Mano's kinship, from his father come.
   And in his mind of gentle chivachie
Otherwise wrought it than in him to raise
Mere unbelief : believe it well did he.
   And knowing Mano's nobleness and praise,
Forthwith from Rouen fast he gan to ride
With all his knights along the woodland ways.
      But when he reached the pile, and stood beside,
He found it fallen in a smouldering heap,
And all who were around away gan glide.
   They would have gone their feast in hall to keep ;
But he bade all stand round, and question made,
Whereof he did a bitter vintage reap.
   He heard both Mano and Diantha paid,
And how that Mano saved them both from pain
By art from Gerbert learned, and magic aid,
   For nought seemed they to smart, it was certain :
But when this thing began to be so said,
Sir Eustace no more silent did remain :
   But like a shadow pale, with bending head,
And weeping bitterly, the true tale told,
How for Diantha was Joanna dead,
   How Mano sped her with the ring of gold,
And how himself the same from her conveyed
To him, from whom she had it first to hold.
      Then, when the love of this unhappy maid
Was manifested to his princely mind,

And all their tragedy abroad displayed,
  Loud wept Duke Richard : neither might he find
A way to ease the sorrow of his heart,
But saved their relics from the scattering wind.
  He bade them gather all, and in good part
To bury them even where that death they died,
Ere from the fatal place he would depart.
  And there a chantry fair he edified,
And his dead brother did with lands endow
Which with him living he could not divide.
  There by the darksome forest stands it now,
And in it is a monument of praise,
Where Mano and Joanna lie in row.
Such sepulchre did good Duke Richard raise.

XVII.—THE END.

I FERGANT, living now my latest days
  Have brought to term this heavy history,
Showing how all things pass, and nothing stays :
  How Fate may mar, and evil destiny.
And my last hand in age and sickness weak
Setting hereto, to God great thanks give I.
  For God hath granted me so far to speak ;
Yea He who showed the purpose to be sought,
Made straight the way, and gave the strength to seek
  That I by serving might be served of thought,
In living might the life of others try,
And at the cost of pain to truth be brought :
  That I might trace the maze of misery,
And make again dead Virtue, noble toil

Rise from the bed of low indignity :
That I from envy's weeds the wasted soil,
Which holds the memory of friends, might clear,
And Falsehood of her vaunting crown despoil :
That I that dreadful age might make appear,
As 'twas in this world's sickness, death, and birth,
Before, and in and forth the thousandth year.

Much have I overpassed in my poor dearth
Of words and memory and method true;
But let me not have failed to heaven and earth
In setting forth with order not undue
The mighty workers of this world's affairs,
Fatality, infinity, these two,
The one the only yoke the other wears.

THE END.

www.ingramcontent.com/pod-product-compliance
Lightning Source LLC
Chambersburg PA
CBHW021729220426
43662CB00008B/766